GHOST STORIES
of the ROCKY MOUNTAINS
Volume II

Barbara Smith

GHOST
HOUSE

Ghost House Books

The Publisher: Ghost House Books
Distributed by Lone Pine Publishing
10145 – 81 Avenue   1808 – B Street NW, Suite 140
Edmonton, AB Canada T6E 1W9   Auburn, WA USA 98001

Website: http://www.ghostbooks.net

National Library of Canada Cataloguing in Publication Data

Smith, Barbara, 1947–
    Ghost stories of the Rocky Mountains, vol. II / Barbara Smith.

    ISBN-13: 97801-894877-21-3
    ISBN-10: 1-894877-21-7

    1. Ghosts—Rocky Mountains. 2. Legends—Rocky Mountains. I. Title.
GR110.R6S64 2003   398.2'097805   C2003-910277-7

Editorial Director: Nancy Foulds
Project Editor: Shelagh Kubish
Illustrations Coordinator: Carol Woo
Production Manager: Gene Longson
Cover Design: Gerry Dotto
Layout & Production: Jeff Fedorkiw

Photo Credits: Every effort has been made to accurately credit photographers. Any errors or omissions should be directed to the publisher for changes in future editions. The photographs in this book are reproduced with the kind permission of the following sources: Bob Campbell (p. 57), Library of Congress (p. 33: USZC4-6668), Jan Jones (p. 45, 48), Robert Smith (p. 78, 81), Barbara Smith (p. 112, 184, 201), Roland Lines, Sr. (p. 163).

The stories, folklore and legends in this book are based on the author's collection of sources including individuals whose experiences have led them to believe they have encountered phenomena of some kind or another. They are meant to entertain, and neither the publisher nor the author claims these stories represent fact.

We acknowledge the financial support of the Government of Canada through the Book Publishing Industry Development Program (BPIDP) for our publishing activities.

PC: P6

For Jo-Anne Christensen,
with love and admiration

CONTENTS

Acknowledgments

It is a privilege and an honor to acknowledge the contributions that the following people have made to this book.

My sincere gratitude goes to the management and staff of Ghost House Books. Special thanks to Grant Kennedy, Shane Kennedy, Nancy Foulds, Shelagh Kubish, Carol Woo, Jeff Fedorkiw and Rick Truppner as well as Ken Davis and Anna Alfonso in the Marketing Department.

I would also like to thank W. Ritchie Benedict of Calgary; Susan Trofaniuk of Edmonton, Alberta; Jan Jones of Edmonton, Alberta; and Bob Campbell of Pueblo, Colorado, for their contributions to this volume.

Introduction

The Rocky Mountains are among the most truly awesome sights in the world. These giant geological features began more than a billion years ago as sediment layers on an ancient seabed. Then, forces deep within the earth's core pushed those sheets from horizontal to vertical. After the strata shifted through the earth's crust, they were exposed to the ravages of the most extreme weather conditions—the ice ages.

Today the range runs some 3000 miles (almost 5000 kilometers) in a roughly north-south direction from the most northerly points of British Columbia, Canada, to New Mexico in the United States.

But those cold facts do not even come close to doing justice to the power of the Rocky Mountains. Their effect on those who see and explore them is one of an almost magic allure and, as a result, a rich heritage of legends has come to revolve around them. This collection, my second book of *Ghost Stories of the Rocky Mountains,* is a sampling of some of those legends as well as ghost stories with a decidedly modern-day twist.

Like all the *Ghost Stories* books I've written, every tale retold in this volume is "true." I put the word "true" in quotation marks because, while I believe in the concept of ghosts, I am also willing to accept that such encounters might have other causes.

There is little that is known for certain about our ethereal world. There are definitely more questions than answers. For instance, are ghosts external or internal to those who encounter them? When a person sees a ghost, has the apparition popped into the reality of the witness or has the observer stepped into a ghost's time and place? I don't believe one explanation will fit all cases. It might be that during those supernatural sightings we are in a time loop, or perhaps we just occasionally become aware of that which we do not normally acknowledge. To my mind, this lack of consistency does not make the experience—or the ghost—any less real. All of these stories have been told to me as real and now I retell them to you with the same attitude.

I do not intend, or wish, to alter anyone's belief system. If reading this book causes you to stop and consider some possible realities that you hadn't previously, then that is fine. In the meantime, though, I do hope that you will be entertained by this book and that you enjoy reading *Ghost Stories of the Rocky Mountains, Volume II*, as much as I have enjoyed writing the book. So, sit back, turn the lights down low and be prepared for some shivers. And always remember, keep your "spirits" up!

1
Haunted Houses

Living near the magnificent Rocky Mountains guarantees that your house is close to some of the finest scenery in the world. As you'll discover when reading the following stories, though, it does not guarantee that your home will be a ghost-free zone.

Eddy's Here

Architecturally, it really wasn't much of a house. That the place was still standing in the 1970s was rather amazing considering that the frame building had been constructed in 1895.

As a home, though, the old wooden structure on East Idaho in Boise, Idaho, was something very special. A man named Church had built the place for his family, and the house served its original purpose admirably well. His five children had been born in the house, and one son had died there. One member of the Church family, daughter Evangeline, lived in the house until she died in 1953.

At that point the property was sold to an entrepreneur named Domingo Adlecoa, who intended to rent it out. He succeeded very well for a very long time. One might even conclude that his rental plan succeeded too well. You see, for nearly 20 years, Domingo's rental house attracted tenant after tenant. The only trouble was, none ever stayed in the place. Some moved out after mere weeks of residency.

Despite the landlord's questioning on the matter, no one ever gave Adlecoa a reason for the sudden departures—at least not a reason associated with the house. One family maintained that a job transfer necessitated a move, while another claimed that a serious illness in the family meant they'd have to live elsewhere. Even at the time, Domingo assumed these explanations were excuses. He suspected that there was something linked to the house itself that was causing the quick turnover in occupants. It wasn't until the 1970s, though, when a forthright and honest woman named Sharon McLusky rented the place for herself and her two children, that he knew what had caused the lack of stability. The old place on East Idaho was haunted. Worse, it was haunted by a very active ghost.

When Sharon found the home for rent at a reasonable rate, she was delighted. She thought the big yard and the number of bedrooms would be ideal for her family. To a large degree, she was right. The family settled in nicely.

After living in the place for a while, though, Sharon began to notice things about herself that she'd never experienced before. She began to have involuntary shivers run through her body. At first she thought those instances occurred randomly, but then she realized that she felt this strange sensation only when she was standing in one particular spot in the house.

One morning, as Sharon went into the kitchen to make breakfast, she thought she saw a shadow of a small person move across the wall opposite her. "No," she said out loud. "That's not possible. No one else is in the room with me. The kids aren't even out of bed yet."

Of course, she was correct, but that knowledge didn't offer Sharon much consolation when moments later she watched as a cupboard door slowly opened and then closed. Deciding that she must not have had nearly as good a sleep as she'd thought she had, Sharon gave her head a shake and tried to get on with the chores at hand.

When her children arrived in the kitchen for breakfast, she subtly asked them if they'd ever noticed anything out of the ordinary in their home. The kids didn't seem to have any idea what their mother was talking about, so rather than risk upsetting them, Sharon let the issue drop. Unfortunately, although she didn't know it at the time, she couldn't keep dropping the issue because the strength of the haunting was increasing dramatically.

In addition to the strange shivers she'd been experiencing, Sharon also began to hear equally strange noises. When a radio came on in an empty room, the woman was decidedly uneasy, but it was the eerie bells that seemed to ring from nowhere and from everywhere at once that really wore on her nerves.

Sharon described this noise as best she could as like "the tinkling of a bell but a bell that sounded like no other bell." The woman was definitely becoming increasingly concerned. At first she tried to tell herself that the ringing sound was caused by an errant string on a musical instrument she kept in the living room. Even as she thought that, though, she knew in her heart that it wasn't the sound of a harp string she had heard.

One night Sharon was awakened by the sound of a phantom voice calling out for help. Shaken, the woman decided to pray for the soul that seemed to be trapped in her house. Over the next few weeks, and then months, there was no further ghostly activity in the house and Sharon optimistically thought that the problem had ended with her prayer. Such was not to be the case.

All was quiet for six months, but then evidence of the haunting recurred with the ringing of the bell. Soon Sharon realized there was a pattern. She heard the disconcerting ringing sound just before other odd things occurred, such as the radio playing, an inexplicable shadow appearing on the wall or doors opening or closing.

Children are usually much more sensitive to supernatural happenings, so it is odd that Sharon's children never mentioned that they had seen or heard or felt anything that puzzled them. Perhaps they merely accepted the strange goings-on as normal for that house, or perhaps they were completely unaware. Whatever the reason, the youngsters seemed to love living in the place, so Sharon was content to stay.

Her conviction was about to be put to a real test. One evening Sharon was napping on the living-room sofa when the sliding doors that divided that room from the next one abruptly shut. Now really frightened, Sharon bolted to her feet. As she did, a series of letters became visible on those closed doors. The woman didn't have time to see if the letters spelled out words because, seconds later, the ball of light that appeared in the room caught her attention. Inside that illuminated globe was a face—the sweetly smiling face of a little boy.

It took Sharon some time to calm herself after this encounter, but once she did, the woman realized that at least she knew she hadn't been imagining anything at all. This house was definitely haunted. It was haunted by the ghost of a little boy. At that point she was actually relieved. Not only did she know for certain that she wasn't losing her mind, but she also knew that the entity was not a threat, that he was just the spirit of a lonely little boy whose soul had somehow become trapped on this earthly plane.

Several nights later, Sharon was entertaining friends—two women and one man. The group had been enjoying a rambling conversation when that same ball of light, complete with the little fellow's smiling face in the center, floated across the room. The glow seemed to bring a cold wind with it, and the flames on the decorative candles burning on a side table suddenly went out. The orb moved quickly and directly to the only man in the room before passing through a wall and out of sight. Needless to say, that marked the end of all non-specific conversation for that night!

Sharon apologized to her guests for the frightening interruption. She tried to explain that she thought the house was haunted but, understandably, her friends were more interested in seeking the safety of their own homes than in listening to anything about a haunting, especially now that they were convinced that this was a *true* ghost story.

Some weeks passed without any evidence of the ghost, and Sharon began to relax. Perhaps, she tried to tell herself, the whole thing had just been a figment of her overactive imagination. Of course, she knew that this wouldn't account for the events her friends witnessed, but it was the best rationalization she could come up with.

Sharon wasn't that scared about living in a house that she knew, in her heart, was haunted because the ghost was that of a child and, more importantly, because her own children seemed completely unbothered by the presence. Unfortunately for the woman's mental and emotional stability, that was about to change.

One morning as Sharon left the house with her son, the boy looked back at the house and excitedly announced, "There's a boy looking out the attic window!" Sharon swung around and followed her son's gaze but saw nothing. She told her son that what he'd seen had merely been an odd reflection of the sun but the child wasn't convinced and, truthfully, neither was his mother. Worse, from that day on, Sharon began to feel decidedly uncomfortable when she was anywhere near the entrance to the attic.

A few days later, Sharon's son came to her. "Come see something, Mom," he urged before taking her to the bottom of the attic stairs and adding the cryptic words, "He died there."

Despite his mother's urgings, the boy never offered any explanation for his assertion. Sharon was no longer feeling comfortable, and she began to think that it was time to move to another house. Perhaps the little phantom was upset by her plans because the haunting became more and more intense. Her son would wake up screaming, saying that he couldn't breathe, that something was choking him.

The following morning when Sharon was alone in the house, she heard a voice call out. It was a child's voice and it seemed to come from nowhere and everywhere. "I'm Eddy," the little voice informed her.

Sharon was now completely terrified—mostly for her son's well-being but for herself and her daughter as well. The soul of this deceased little boy had, she was sure, invaded her family's home. Or, had they in fact invaded his home? Whichever, she knew she'd have to do something—fast. The young mother began to investigate the history of her rented home and discovered that a boy named Edmond had once been associated with the house. Sharon was convinced that this was the child whose spirit haunted the house.

Not many days later Sharon is sure she saw Eddy's complete image, and that time, he was not alone. Sharon went into a room in the attic that she rarely used, except for storage. As she walked through the doorway she saw two people in the room—a woman and a little boy. The images were so clear that, at first, she thought they were real people. When the figures disappeared before her eyes, though, she knew that the people she had seen were actually ghosts.

That evening, as the stressed woman decided to treat herself to a hot, relaxing bath, at least one of the spirits made its presence known again. Sharon turned off the light in the bathroom and, for a few minutes, lay in a tub full of comfortably warm water. Then, without warning, the light came back on and the water in the tub "turned icy cold."

Sharon called a friend of hers. She knew that this woman, named Judy, was extraordinarily sensitive to paranormal situations and could give a psychic opinion about the house. Judy came over and immediately confirmed Eddy's identity but assured Sharon that the child's ghost was absolutely harmless. Unfortunately, Judy saw more than just Eddy. She also saw the ghost of an old man. He was confined to bed and, apparently, was not a nice person at all.

This news made Sharon admit that she was just about at the end of her ability to live under such circumstances, especially as she was the only adult in the house. Because her children were adamant that they did not want to move, rather than find another house to lease, she decided to import other adults into the home by renting out a couple of the spare rooms.

Some of her tenants were happy with the arrangement, but the man living in the attic was uncomfortable right from the first night. Sharon had warned the man that the area he was living in was haunted and, at first, he thought that her cautionary words had merely caused his imagination to work overtime. Despite his attempts to rationalize his discomfort, the man was ready to move out when fate, or the ghosts, made up his mind for him. In the early morning of a winter's day in 1972, the man awoke to find his room and everything in it on fire.

Flames blocked the door, and in order to save his own life he took the only escape available to him—he jumped out the window. He spent several days in the hospital recovering from the injuries he suffered as a result of the three-story fall.

The fire damaged the house so badly that the owner decided the place was not worth repairing. Demolition of that old haunted house on East Idaho in Boise was planned for March 15, the Ides of March, in 1973.

A few days before that, Sharon McLusky moved from the haunted house. Moving is rarely pleasant, but moving away from ghosts is apparently worse. It seems that a man helping her with the move fell to the bottom of the basement stairs. After the plunge he was adamant that a broken stair had caused the mishap. But there was no broken stair. This accident occurred seconds after he had teased Sharon about her conviction that the place was haunted. It seems that not even the dead like to have their presence denied.

The McLusky family soon found adequate, and unhaunted, accommodation elsewhere. This leaves the question of the ghosts. We know that they did not follow Sharon and her children to their new place. Where could they have gone? Perhaps, as we have no indication to the contrary, we should just presume that Eddy, the woman and the angry old man have finally gone to their eternal reward.

Huge and Haunted

Right from the beginning, there was little question that the enormous home on Holter Street in Helena, Montana, was haunted. And after the family that bought the place in 1969 researched its history and found out about the original owner, the identity of the ghost was not a mystery either. Between those two points, though, lies an amazing ghost story.

In the 1880s, Judge Theodore Brantly moved west from Tennessee. Although he was only 25 years old at the time, he already considered himself a failure. After all, even though he was well educated and had been given substantial career opportunities, he had not made a success of himself. He was determined to start over again in Montana. This time he would work harder and, no matter what the cost, he would succeed. The man worked night and day. Not only did the judge's health suffer, but his relationship with his family did as well. Although he died wealthy, he died far too young and having spent almost no time with his children. One would like to think that, given the opportunity to live his life over again, he would change his ways. As the following story reveals, though, Judge Brantly never changed his behavior—even after death.

In the early spring of 1969, the Card family bought an enormous old house on Holter Street. The place had clearly once been a spectacular showpiece of opulence but had fallen into disrepair and been divided into apartment suites. The Cards planned to refurbish the grand old place and return the once-luxurious family home to its original grandeur. The couple loved everything about the house. They loved the generous look of the oak trim, the leaded glass windows and especially the carved sidewalk block in front of the house. "Brantly" the inscription read, as this property they'd just purchased had been the house of Judge Theodore Brantly.

Dorothy and Bob Card, along with their son and daughter, moved into one of the suites in the house before they began the massive renovations. They lived quiet and happy lives there until 1973, by which time they had compiled the resources necessary to begin the work. From that moment on they became more than aware that the former owner, Judge Brantly, had retained a lively interest in the home he had built so many years before.

His ghostly presence became almost palpable. According to Dorothy Card, there was an atmosphere of "unrest" throughout the residence. While alone in the house, she had heard the big heavy front door slam shut. She called out the names of her family members, thinking that one of them had come home. When no one replied, she started to the front hall to investigate. At the moment she was walking down the stairs, she could clearly hear someone coming up. Unfortunately, she couldn't see anyone. When something seemed to brush by her at a midpoint on the staircase she was extremely startled. All her senses, except her sight, told her that she was not alone.

At first Dorothy was hesitant to share her strange experience with the other members of her family, but after a few days she summoned sufficient courage to introduce the subject to them. Her children were especially glad she was so candid, for they too had experienced identical, inexplicable sounds and feelings at times when their parents had been out for the evening. Even though their son had been especially terrified whenever he'd heard the invisible intruder, the kids had resisted the temptation to tell their parents for fear of upsetting them.

The ghostly visitations were always the same. The front door would open and close before heavy footfalls marched up the staircase. Though these noises were real, no one ever saw any image in conjunction with them.

Next the Cards began to hear footsteps pounding across the floor of the attic, which had been completely inaccessible for some time. No one in the house at that time—no one living, that is—had any idea how to reach the attic space. As well, the Cards' televisions would operate quite independently, even turning on while no one was in the house—a sure sign of a ghostly presence.

It wasn't long before these events began to disturb the family's happy existence, and they started to inquire about Theodore Brantly. They were told that it was always late when the judge came home from work, and that it was his habit to go directly upstairs but not to bed. He was an insomniac who usually spent most of the night pacing around the house worrying about the court cases he had before him at the time.

The judge may not have been a man who enjoyed life very much but, in death, he did seem to have at least one fun-loving quality—he would eat any candy left out in the house that was once his.

Over the years the Cards became accustomed to sharing their house with the man who'd originally invested in it. They were never able to finish all the renovations they'd planned, and, for reasons having nothing to do with the haunting, they sold the place in 1977.

Some months later, Dorothy was called back to her former home. A package had been delivered to her at the old address. When she and the current owner began chatting, it became clear to Mrs. Card that the tenacious entity had stayed on. Those owners also moved—after seeing a very large potted plant in their living room rise a few feet above the floor and move about in a strange shaking motion before falling back to the ground.

This action terrified both the husband and wife because no one had been near the plant at the time. Not knowing what else they could do about the bizarre occurrence, the pair simply got up to clean up the mess. The pot started to move away from them. Seconds later the plant withered and died. The couple moved out of the house as soon as they could.

The next owners, whom we'll call the Joneses, were not so communicative. By deduction, though, it's obvious that they were well aware that their house was haunted. They have been quoted as saying that if there were ghosts in their house they were *their* ghosts. The Joneses were apparently determined to keep all information about their paranormal housemate to themselves.

It is equally apparent that, so far, Judge Theodore Brantly's residence in Helena, Montana, has been a supernaturally lengthy one.

Phantom Footsteps

"You know, of course, that the house is haunted?"

Those words greeted Karl Vogel, a highly skilled and deeply skeptical craftsman, as he worked refurbishing a 33-room mansion just outside Denver, Colorado.

In fact Karl hadn't known that he had been working in the company of a ghost. He did know that he wasn't at all interested in listening to the visitor's nonsense—even if the man *was* the former caretaker at the palatial estate and therefore familiar with the property. All Karl cared about was getting on with the job at hand.

Karl's visitor did not seem to sense the worker's feelings, though, because he carried on about the subject.

"Yes, this house is definitely haunted," the older man continued. "It's haunted by at least one ghost and I can show you physical proof of that fact. Some years ago, just before she died, the former owner, my employer, instructed that when she died her body be laid out by the fireplace in the Great Hall. She said that once her remains were resting in that beautiful spot she would send a message to the living."

Although Karl pretended not to be interested, he was intrigued by what this elderly man was saying and he listened carefully as the former caretaker explained the old woman's plan to indicate that her soul had survived. She had told friends and relatives alike that she would put a visible split in a ceiling beam directly above where her corpse had been set.

The elderly man acknowledged that such things as activity caused from beyond the grave are indeed difficult for us to understand, but that the woman's spirit had carried out exactly what her living self had promised. As soon as the casket was rolled in front of the fireplace, a loud cracking sound came from above the heads of those present. Everyone in the room, the former caretaker included, looked up. Impossibly, a main beam directly above them had a large split in it. The crack ran lengthwise along the beam but did not extend to either end.

After he had delivered his ghostly gossip, the older man bid Karl a good day and left the house. For a while, Karl worked on the difficult area that was taking his attention that day, but after a time his curiosity got the best of him and he walked into the Great Hall. The older man had been correct. There was a long split in the wooden support.

Karl stared at the anomaly for a while before deciding that the beam's being cracked did not mean that the elderly man had been telling the truth or that the house was haunted. Right after that visit, he had to admit that he felt a little uneasy. Soon he was back to being relaxed and busy on the job because the palatial, and possibly haunted, house had been purchased by the Bradleys, a wealthy family eager to move there from the city.

The Bradleys had hired Karl and also enrolled their three sons in the local school. Unfortunately, although the family owned the property, they were not yet living there, and school board regulations dictated that the children must be staying in the house to be considered residents of the area and therefore able to attend a local school.

Dr. Bradley, the children's father, made arrangements to move into his "new" house and to stay there on certain days of the week. He wasn't able to be there every night, though, so he asked Karl Vogel, the trusted worker, if he could help out by staying in the home with the boys on the nights that neither of the parents could be there. Karl kindly agreed.

As for the Bradley boys, they needed no coaxing to be convinced that living in an enormous deserted house in the woods was going to be a good time. They packed their bags and got ready quickly. Although they didn't know it then, they were getting ready to experience a time they would never forget.

The first night Karl stayed with the boys, they set up camp in one room. Though there were dozens of rooms in the house, only the one was habitable. Shortly after the children fell asleep, Karl decided that he, too, should turn in. Just at that instant he heard the back door open and then slam closed. At first he presumed it was just Dr. or Mrs. Bradley coming in.

He sat and listened as footsteps slid along the floors below. The soft sounds did not vary but "walked" from the back door to a main-floor room and then another. Still, Karl was not concerned. He merely waited quietly for whoever had arrived to call up to the bedroom and identify himself or herself. That call never came. Instead, after some time, the back door opened and slammed closed for a second time and then, once again, there was silence in the house.

Karl got up and looked outside to see who had been so inconsiderate. There was no one there, no one anywhere on the grounds near the house. Because there was only one approach to the house—a half-mile long driveway—

he was sure that he would be able see the person leave. But there was no one there.

I must have been dreaming, Karl said to himself. He knew for certain that he'd heard a person come into the house, walk around on the main floor and then leave. He decided that he would definitely address the issue with his employer the next day. At that, the man lay back down in bed and eventually drifted off to sleep.

The next day he asked the homeowner about the situation. The man denied having been anywhere near the house anytime after dark. Neither party was pleased with the conversation but rather than get into a senseless argument, they dropped the discussion.

All was quiet in the house for the next few nights. Then, again when Karl was staying overnight, the pattern repeated itself. He was just getting ready to close his eyes when he heard the back door open and slam closed. This time, as soon as he could hear the footsteps shuffling into a room far from any exterior door, Karl made his move. Determined to catch the trespasser, he jumped out of bed and hurried down the stairs.

The sounds of the footsteps were still distinct—he was able to follow their progress through the huge old place. Better still, the light from a full moon shone in the windows and lit the area so Karl was able to see. There was no one—visible—anywhere in the house. But the sounds of a person walking about continued.

Instantly, Karl's skepticism dissolved and he knew exactly what was walking around the house that he was charged with overseeing. It was not a person at all. It was a ghost. More specifically, it was the ghost of the former owner—the ghost that the elderly man had told him about some weeks before. Nervously, Karl called out to the entity that had disturbed his peace of mind.

"I'm just trying to restore your beautiful home. If you don't want me to continue the work just tell me now, and I'll stop."

No voice answered Karl, but he could hear sounds of footsteps once again. They were retreating toward the door. Seconds later he heard the back door open and slam closed again. After that the nights were quiet in the huge old Colorado country home and Karl Vogel was a firm believer in life after death.

Shortly after that incident, the entire family moved into the house. Dr. Bradley had always enjoyed getting up early in the morning to have the house to himself for a while before the others woke up. This routine became even more important to him since moving to the enormous heritage home.

It was during one of these mornings that the physician came to believe in paranormal events, just as Karl Vogel had. Bradley was alone in the drawing room of his mansion. All was quiet—until an ornament lifted up from a nearby table and floated about a foot and a half in mid-air before setting itself down again. Seconds later the object fell over on its side and didn't move again.

The man was sure one of his sons was responsible for the incident and he rushed out to find the culprit. He found the boys, but they most certainly could not be blamed for the trick because they were fast asleep in their rooms.

On a weekend day some weeks later the entire Bradley family went into town on a shopping trip. They returned several hours later to find that one room of the house had been completely trashed. All the plants in that room had been pulled from their pots before someone or something had turned the pots of soil upside down on the floor. At first they were sure that someone had broken into the place, but there were no signs of a burglary and nothing was missing. No one was ever able to find a reason for that mysterious, messy occurrence.

Whatever force had tampered with the plants was apparently not finished. That evening as the family sat watching television, a single leaf on one of the many plants in the room where they were sitting started to move. Not even one other leaf on any of the other trees or plants in the room was moving, and there was no draft. There wasn't much in the way of a reasonable explanation for this oddity, either.

The Bradleys were intrigued by this surprising feature of their new home. They began to research not only psychic phenomena but also the history of the house. They discovered that the house had last been owned by an elderly woman who ultimately died in the house. They also learned about poltergeists, noisy and active ghosts that are rarely seen. These were good pieces of information for Robert and Dorothy Bradley to have because poltergeist-like tricks were what their resident phantom had in store for the couple.

They would constantly find lights on that they knew they'd recently turned off. The house had just been rewired, so they called the electrician back. He could not understand what was causing this annoying situation. In order to be thorough, though, he cut open a panel in one of the walls and hauled out some electrical cord. What he found was nothing short of shocking. The cords that he'd carefully braided together just weeks before were all separated. That discovery did nothing to alleviate the problem, of course. In fact, it caused more concern.

Further research into the house's former owners might have supplied the answer to the questions about the unreliable lights. It seems that one couple who'd lived in the mansion some years before were not on good terms with one another. They fought constantly—mostly about lights being either on or off. She, apparently, liked the house to be dark even during the day. He preferred brightness. They frequently went about flicking the light switches to whatever position they were individually comfortable with.

As the lights became more and more of a problem, the Bradleys theorized that it was the ghosts of those former owners haunting the place that used to be their home. The Bradleys became convinced that the phantom maneuvers were always connected to a future occurrence in life. They felt that the ghost's presence was a harbinger of short-term ill with, fortunately, never any lingering aftereffects. The couple was so convinced that their analysis of this pattern was correct that they wrote an entire book (*Psychic Phenomena: Revelations and Experiences*) about their situation.

Although they never actually saw an apparition in their home, other people did. After they had been settled in the house for a few years, the Bradleys offered tours of their unusual and enormous home in return for donations to charities. Many of the people who came to walk through the house saw ghostly images either staring out of windows or floating from room to room.

Eventually the amount of work involved in owning a 33-room house began to outweigh the fun, and they sold their mansion—ghosts and all. The people who bought the place from the Bradleys apparently didn't have the temperament necessary to live in a haunted house, for not long after, they moved out. Unfortunately that update from the mid-1990s is the last report we have about the house.

We can only hope that everyone, the living and the dead, are currently peacefully sharing the huge, historic home.

Lonely Wraith

Some years ago, Jane Brakhage explained to a journalist with the *Rocky Mountain News* that she'd had an intriguing experience.

As she told the journalist, Brakhage had been awakened in her Rollinsville, Colorado, home by a little boy standing beside her bed. You might wonder if such news was worth reporting, especially as Brakhage was the mother of five children—some of them boys. In this case, though, the incident definitely was worthy of note, for the "boy" whose presence awoke her was not human.

Jane Brakhage explained that at first she presumed her little visitor that morning was one of her own children. She soon found out, though, that her initial assessment was dead wrong. The "boy" standing beside the bed was certainly no relation to her. He was not even from her time, but it was clear that he needed to be mothered.

The waif stood just inches from her face and stared at Jane in the moonlit room before telling her that he was not feeling well. Jane sat up in bed, but as she did, the little fellow moved away from her. No matter how she coaxed, the skinny boy in raggedy clothes simply would not come to her. Seconds later, the woman got out of bed and walked across the room to the boy's side. As she put her arms out to the lad he disappeared—simply vanished before her eyes.

Although that encounter startled the woman, it also helped to explain a strange incident that Crystal, one of her daughters, had experienced while the family was tobogganing at a local hill.

All four of Crystal's siblings were at the bottom of the slope. Crystal was at the top. She was enjoying the moment far too much to have noticed that she was alone, and so, in timeless childhood tradition, the girl yelled out for someone to give her a start down the hill. Almost immediately, Crystal's request was honored when a firm hand on her back pushed her down the snowy hillside. She giggled in delight as she zipped along aboard the wooden toboggan to the bottom of the slope.

As she brushed herself off and told her brothers and sisters what a great slide she'd had, Crystal looked up to the top of the hill. There was no one there. All her siblings had stayed at the bottom waiting for her to join them. Perhaps the phantom hand that had helped her have such a good time had belonged to that little boy's ghost. If so, let's hope that his spirit also enjoyed the afternoon of sledding—before he had taken ill again as his physical body had many, many years before.

Even in death, one might suppose, it would be comforting for a child to have a caring adult to come to him and an appreciative child to play with.

Founders' Phantoms

In 1844, after Joseph Smith, founder of the Mormon Church, was murdered in western Illinois, the newly formed religious group would have been leaderless had it not been for the direction provided by a young church affiliate—Brigham Young. Young took over Smith's role as leader and successfully guided the sect's trek west in search of a place to live in peace. When they reached what is now Salt Lake City in Utah, it was prophetically announced "this is the place," and the small fellowship settled in. Over the years their numbers flourished until the Church of the Latter Day Saints became as established as it is today.

Fortunately, physical evidence of the community's pioneering days has been preserved for people to visit. According to promotional material about the area, "This Is The Place Heritage Park…is a living community that has been painstakingly restored or recreated to represent Utah's past." Some of the original buildings still exist.

Even more interesting for our purposes, metaphysical evidence also remains—ghosts. The spirits of several of those who lived and died in the mid-1800s have never left the site. As a result, many visitors to the area are convinced that the place is very haunted.

The spirit of Brigham Young himself reportedly haunted his original farmhouse for many years. When the

Ann Eliza Webb, one of Brigham Young's former wives, still haunts a historic farmhouse in Salt Lake City, Utah.

building was moved to its current location in a historical park, Young's ghost left the building, but the home continued to be haunted by the manifestation of Young's 19th wife, Ann Eliza Webb.

That second haunting is even more of a mystery than the presence of Young's ghost because long before her death, Webb divorced Young and made a career of publicly condemning both the man and the church he led.

Despite Ann Eliza Webb's hatred for Brigham Young and all he represented, her ghost has been seen at the dining-room window of the old Young homestead. She is easily recognized by her tiny stature and severe black clothing.

The spirit of Mary Fielding Smith, widow of Joseph Smith, has also remained in her home. She is said to be a cranky phantom and is most often seen shaking her fist or wagging her finger at the outside world as she stands in the doorway of what had been her last earthly residence.

Fortunately, not all the paranormal residents are can-tankerous. In a nearby house tourists have enjoyed the sounds of children laughing and playing in and around the building, even though it is empty. The park where these buildings stand is open to the public for those who are interested in experiencing living history.

Little Sir Echo

Hinton, Alberta, is a small town just east of Jasper in the Rocky Mountain foothills. This location means that Hinton might not remain a small town for long, but at least one soul, a ghost named Echo, will not be there to see the community's growth.

A woman named Marie explained that Echo was a part of life in her household from the time her daughter, Kaitlyn, was just a baby. Once Kaitlyn was old enough to talk, she explained to her mother that the spirit of Echo had been with her for as long as she could remember. Echo's presence is gone now, but to this day, Marie remains grateful for the being's loyalty to her daughter.

"He was a wonderful spirit," Marie explained. "Kaitlyn called him her guardian angel."

Marie continued, "If it hadn't been for Echo looking out after my daughter, I dread to think what might have happened to Kaitlyn. He protected her from harm."

Kaitlyn was only an infant when she and her mother first realized that something very unusual had joined their lives.

"When Kaitlyn was very young she would always seem to be following something around with her eyes. Whatever it was she was watching never upset her or anything; actually, it made her happy. She would smile at it a lot. The entity was invisible to us so we never knew what it was she was looking at," Marie recalled before adding, "When my daughter was about two years of age she started talking to someone all the time—someone none of the adults in her life could see. We simply shrugged it off as Kaitlyn having an imaginary friend as so many children that age do."

This imaginary friend showed amazing abilities. Marie stated, "Kaitlyn would keep a conversation going with her invisible companion. Although we could only ever hear one side of the conversation, it was more than evident that she thought she was talking to someone."

Of course, Marie's curiosity was piqued. "We asked her on many occasions who she was talking to and she always said 'I am talking to Echo.' We asked her if that was her imaginary friend, and she said no, that he was not imaginary at all but followed her wherever she went."

With the simplicity of a child, Kaitlyn declared, "Echo is a ghost."

Marie, of course, was not a child and looked at life from a more complex perspective. "We didn't fully believe her. We shrugged it off as a creation of her imagination."

As many parents would, Marie presumed that this stage was just one of many Kaitlyn would go through as she grew up. If this presumption was correct, then it was a very long stage!

"Through the years, as Kaitlyn was growing up, she always had this Echo person with her. She said he stayed in her room with her and that he talked to her all the time."

Although they eventually found out that Echo was haunting them for a very serious reason, he could be something of a practical joker.

"He used to turn the lights in my basement suite on. The bathroom was just across from my bedroom so when he turned that light on it would shine at my eyes and wake me up."

The first time this happened Marie didn't give it a second thought. She just presumed that Kaitlyn had been up to go to the bathroom. When she checked, though, the mother discovered her daughter fast asleep, right beside her in bed. To confirm that there was no chance the child had slipped out of bed and back without Marie noticing, the girl's mother explained that they shared a water bed so were each aware even when the other rolled over.

When Kaitlyn was four years old, the family moved from one house to another. Marie stated simply, "Echo came with us. Kaitlyn would play with him for hours on end. I would listen to her conversation and it was like she was talking to someone who wasn't there. I worried about it a lot but then just thought that, being a child, she had an overactive imagination."

Of course, while this unique haunting was progressing, so was life with all its distractions and complications. As their new home was going to be more expensive to maintain, Marie began to look around for a roommate to live with them. It didn't take long to find someone, and soon after Kaitlyn and Marie moved into the new place, so did a man we'll call Al.

Marie recalled that just days after Al moved in, Kaitlyn came to her mother "with a worried look on her face. She said 'Mommy, Echo thinks we should move. He says I am not safe here.' "

Now Echo really had Marie's attention! She decided to probe. "I asked her more about this Echo person. I asked her if she really saw someone there. She assured me she did. I asked Kaitlyn to tell me more about Echo. She said he was the ghost of a really nice 10-year-old boy who kept her company all the time. She said he died a long time ago—sometime in the 1940s."

Marie continued, "Now, being a four-year-old, she wouldn't have known about dates that long ago, so she definitely had my attention. I didn't think she was making this up. She said he was born in the late 1930s or early 1940s on November 15th. I asked her how he died, and she told me he had drowned in a lake in the springtime in the 1940s. She described him as having brown hair, brown eyes and a darker complexion. She also told me that his mother, father and his sister, Sarah, died in a car crash some years after he had died."

Marie was utterly amazed at the details her daughter was supplying. Wanting to ascertain as surely as possible that Kaitlyn was safe with the paranormal companion, Marie probed further.

"I asked her if she was ever scared of him but she just kind of looked at me funny and said, 'No Mom, he would never hurt me. He is my friend.' "

Unfortunately, this warm and supportive situation changed drastically one evening. Marie explained, "When I put Kaitlyn to bed on this one particular night she was arguing with someone. I assumed it was 'Echo.' A few minutes later she yelled for me so I ran upstairs and asked her what was wrong. She was upset and very tired. She said Echo wouldn't stop talking and that she wanted to be able to get to sleep. I didn't know how to handle it so I asked her what she wanted me to do. She told me to put Echo in another room because all she wanted to do was fall asleep."

Perhaps feeling a little foolish, Marie did "put" her daughter's invisible longtime companion in another room. Kaitlyn immediately fell fast asleep.

Marie settled down for a quiet evening playing computer games. "The computer was in the basement. In the room immediately above it, on the main floor, was a door to the outside. I heard little footsteps by the door and figured my Kaitlyn was up but I checked, there was no one there and the door was still locked. Then I went upstairs to the bedroom to check on Kaitlyn. She was still fast asleep."

Marie's practical nature came to the fore. "I told myself I'd just heard the house creaking."

That might have worked for that instance but when the pattern continued, Marie had to admit that there was something more happening. Even Al, the roommate, began to notice the sounds of footsteps at times when, logically, there should not have been any.

Not wanting to scare away her tenant, Marie just joked about the noises. "He would always think that someone had come into the house but I just told him not to worry, that it was just our ghost."

Oddly, that seemed to calm the man down.

For the next few weeks the phantom footsteps continued but everyone simply accepted them. Even if they were puzzling, at least by now they were routine.

That pattern continued until the day Kaitlyn confronted her mother with the following startling statement: "Echo says we have to move, that if we stay here something bad is going to happen."

Of course, this news really frightened Marie. In January, when Kaitlyn broke her arm while tobogganing, the girl's mother figured that the prediction must have come true. But the prophecy was not fulfilled that easily, and even after the sledding accident the little girl continued to maintain that Echo was saying they had to move.

Marie wondered if perhaps Kaitlyn simply didn't like this new house. Finally, on a horrible evening when Marie had to be out of the house for a while to help her sister, Kaitlyn and Marie both found out what Echo's warnings had been about.

"When I came home my daughter was waiting up for me. She said she needed to talk to me. She brought me into my room where she told me that my roommate had tried to hurt her. Apparently Echo somehow helped her get away from him. She and Echo waited together in my bedroom with the door locked till I got home."

Now Marie understood. "I guess that is what Echo meant about Kaitlyn not being safe."

Marie, of course, ordered the man out of the house immediately. But, even though Echo's purpose for remaining among the living had now been accomplished, he continued to linger on this plane.

"Not long after I kicked my roommate out, I had a friend over. She and I were downstairs in the basement when we heard footsteps on the floor over our heads. She thought this was strange because we were alone in the house. Of course, I was well used to Echo and his antics by this time. She said, 'There's someone in the house,' but I told her, 'No, that's just our ghost.' She laughed at me and said I was crazy. I told her to go search around upstairs. When she came back downstairs, she was as white as a ghost."

When she was able to find her voice, Marie's friend said, "No one is up there."

Marie smiled. "I told you, it's just our ghost. His name is Echo."

That was the end of the friend's visit. Marie recalled, "She made me drive her home and she swore she would never come to my house again. She was really scared."

What was more important, though, was that Kaitlyn and Marie were so entirely comfortable with Echo. The lack of a roommate, however, did necessitate moving once more.

"Echo again followed us to our new place. Echo was obviously still with us. I would still hear his footsteps.

After a few months, though, the footsteps stopped and Kaitlyn stopped talking to Echo."

The absence of their long-term ethereal friend made Marie just as curious as the ghost's presence had. "I asked Kaitlyn how come she never talked to Echo anymore. She told me that he had left because she was safe now and that he had to go on to help other kids who needed him.

"Kaitlyn is eight years old now, and Echo has been gone for about two years now. She still remembers him very well, as do I."

Judging from their fond memories of the years they were haunted by the little boy's ghost, it would seem that they actually miss his presence.

"We didn't have any of the unpleasantness associated with a haunting. No bad smells or anything like that. Echo was a great ghost. We were never scared and he never tried to harm us in any way. I think Echo was just a boy who was sent back to earth to look after other kids. I do thank Echo for being around. That roommate went on to hurt another child very badly. Without Echo protecting Kaitlyn, I don't know what might have happened that night when I was at my sister's."

The story of Echo, Kaitlyn and Marie might cause a person to pause and consider what might have been the true nature of their own "imaginary friends" from childhood.

Warm Springs Spirit

In 1913, Dr. Carl Hill, a physician at Boise, Idaho's St. Luke's Hospital, built a house on Warm Springs Avenue. At the time it was one of the most extravagant homes in the fledgling city—rumored to have cost close to $5000. Hill must have been easily able to afford this luxury, for he lived in the palatial residence for many years. Hill died in 1930 and almost immediately after his death, the doctor returned to the Warm Springs Avenue address—as a ghost.

Even though the supernatural was not widely popular during the Dirty Thirties, this haunting was well accepted by neighbors. The ghost did not bother them at all because they knew that it was only Dr. Hill's spirit returning to spend his afterlife at the residence he'd had built.

By the late 1970s the former Hill House was still haunted and had also become rundown. Renovations were begun to restore the old home to its former grandeur. As is commonly the case with such restoration work, the process increased the intensity of the ghostly activity. The new owners reported hearing shuffling footsteps coming from different rooms of the house—rooms that were known to be empty at the time. The attic door would not stay shut no matter how often or how forcefully it was closed.

These owners, whom we shall refer to here as Rog and Shar Swan, must have been very accepting because they were never upset by the phantom sounds or sights. Soon neighbors advised the couple that the ghost in their home was not a new phenomenon but had been a fixture there for many years. This news delighted the Swans, who were pleased that they had apparently captured even more of a piece of history than they'd originally bargained for.

The couple never believed the tales that the ghost in their house was the spirit of a bootlegger who had owned the place after Dr. Hill. Right from the beginning they were pleased to be absolutely certain that "their" ghost was the soul of the long-deceased doctor.

To assure the late Dr. Hill that they were happy to have his spirit in residence, Rog and Shar began including the presence in their conversations. They were so hospitable that they even put a special rocking chair in the attic so that the phantom could rest his weary, and slightly transparent, image into eternity.

With such welcoming flesh-and-blood homeowners as roommates, it's likely that Dr. Hill's ghost still haunts Warm Springs Avenue. May it keep his soul happy to spend his afterlife happily sitting and rocking in the attic of the house he so loved in life.

Free-Range Phantoms

Some ghost stories are difficult to verify, but this one required little external verification because I've known Joan for many years. She is an honest and forthright person who holds a responsible job with the police department in a large city. In short, Joan is a woman who can be trusted.

In the mid-1980s Joan and her friend Irene set out on an adventure. They were driving to the most northerly part of the Rocky Mountains, in British Columbia, to visit Joan's sister Pat and brother-in-law Mike.

As Joan explained, Pat and Mike "live on an open-range cattle ranch nestled in the Rockies. The ranch is an amazing place. They have over 3000 acres [about 1200 hectares] in God's country."

By most standards their property is both enormous and isolated. As Joan explained, the nearest neighbor is about 2 miles (3.5 kilometers) away. "Mike's father originally settled the land. He was a Scottish immigrant who endeavored to live as far away from civilization as he could."

Over the years the family has built various structures on the property as more shelters were needed. Today, even the very first building, a trading post, still stands. By now, Joan explained, there are also "several homes on the property. The largest one is fairly new. Mike and his siblings built it as a present for their aging parents. The smaller house, separated from the parent's home by a stream, was Pat and Mike's."

The extended rural family enjoyed their living arrangements and often hosted visits from other relatives. "Over the years, family members would go and spend

Deep in the Canadian Rockies, two friends discovered that natural beauty doesn't scare away stubborn ghosts.

time up at the ranch to shake away the cobwebs of city life and to enjoy the fresh country air."

During two of Joan and Irene's visits there, Joan got more of a change than she had bargained for. Her first unusual experience occurred in the larger house. "Mike's father had passed away and his Mom had moved to town, leaving the house vacant for a short time. We traveled up in early October with the weather was already starting to turn cold. The day we arrived, we caught up on family news and dined with Pat and Mike in their warm little home. That night, when it came time to turn in, Irene and

I made our way, with the aid of flashlights, over the stream to the big house. We chose bedrooms across the hall from one another and began to settle in with our luggage."

It was late by the time the pair had unpacked and organized themselves. Even though they were both tired from the long drive, neither woman felt ready to sleep, so they decided to chat for a while. "As we sat talking about the day, we suddenly heard three distinct, loud knocks on the front door. It was 11 PM. That's late for farming folk to be up and about, so I assumed that it was Mike coming over to bring some extra blankets to chase away the chill."

Joan remembers that she called out "Come on in!" but received no answer.

After a pause to collect her thoughts, the woman continued, "There was silence. Then we heard the sound of dishes being rattled in the kitchen cupboards. It sounded as if someone had come in and was starting to prepare a meal!"

Joan and Irene could only look at one another in disbelief. A second later they realized that they hadn't heard the door open. If there was someone downstairs, how did the person get in?

Not timid, Joan decided to investigate. "I stuck my head outside the bedroom door. The sounds of dishes rattling stopped immediately. I had a clear view of the kitchen and there was not a soul in sight!"

Joan demonstrated her pragmatic nature as she continued, "We were pretty amazed, but it had been a long day, [and we'd] driven for over seven hours. The feather pillows were calling our names, so we each retired to our own bedrooms for the night."

Seconds later, they realized that the sleep they both wanted so desperately was not going to come easily.

"All night long, the heavy footsteps of an adult male walked the hallway, back and forth, passing both of our bedrooms. As tired as we were, with all that had happened, those phantom footfalls meant it took a long while to finally drop off to sleep."

Although they were definitely disturbed by the noises, neither Joan nor Irene was frightened because they had a pretty good idea what was happening.

"One of Mike's brothers had met with a tragic, untimely demise. His belongings were stored in the house in a small bedroom at the end of the hallway."

To this day, they are sure he was the invisible entity in the house with them that night. They knew that they were staying in what had been his lifelong home and that his ghost would do them no harm. The next few days of their stay were quiet. The last night they were there, though, "at precisely 11 PM, there were three distinct, loud knocks at the front door once more! I looked at Irene and she looked back at me," Joan recalled. "I said to her, 'I don't know about you, but I'm not inviting him in again this time!' "

The noisy ghost, it seems, was willing to respect their wishes. "It was quiet all night. We had a great sleep!"

Several years later Irene and Joan returned to Pat and Mike's Rocky Mountain home. This time, they also brought Irene's fiancé, Larry, and longtime friend Chuck with them. Pat and Mike had moved from the small house to the big one, leaving the smaller one vacant and available for overnight guests to use.

Intent on a relaxing mountain holiday, Joan and her friend Irene had no idea how many unsettling experiences were in store for them.

Joan recalled, "The first night we all settled in. Irene and Larry shared a bedroom, I took my nephew's old bedroom and Chuck bunked down on the floor in the living room. Right from the start we heard light, feminine footsteps in the house at about 2 AM."

Perhaps feeling responsible for her friends' well-being during their visit to her sister's home, Joan responded immediately. "I called out to Chuck asking if it was him walking around. He was fast asleep. I got up from bed and peered out into the darkness of the living room but could see no one, save for Chuck on the floor in his sleeping bag. Irene had heard me call out and confirmed that she had also heard the soft footsteps but had not been wandering about.

"The next night, we again enjoyed the company of family and friends over supper. When it came time to head over to the small house, we made our way back over the stream. I was the first one to go into the living room," Joan remembered.

As soon as she did, she stopped dead in her tracks. There before her was the image of a young woman sitting on an armchair.

"She was sitting with her legs up and to the side, gazing thoughtfully out of the picture window beside her. She was very slender of build, dressed in a light dress and had long, dark hair. As soon as the others entered the room she simply faded from sight! Around 2 AM, though, the sounds of footsteps started again."

With a chuckle, Joan recalled her reaction—"This time I didn't bother to look out of my room. I knew it wasn't Chuck!"

What a good thing that staying in a haunted house didn't bother Joan, because the ghostly activity was far from over. Her next experience would likely have driven a less calm woman screaming into the night!

"On the third night, we were all sleeping soundly when I got the distinct feeling that I was not alone in bed. I always sleep on my left side and this night I could feel the length of a body snuggled close from behind, like a child would sleep with a parent. I could even feel the hair of this 'other person' on my neck and back. Knowing that I had gone to bed by myself, I closed my eyes tightly, offered a prayer for this lost soul and then ordered it to get out of my bed! The spirit took some convincing because it was a good 10 or 15 minutes before the sensation of not being alone in bed dissipated."

Once the manifestation had gone, Joan felt considerably better, but the spirit, it seemed, was not pleased. "No sooner had I dropped back off to sleep than there came a most horrendous 'bang.' At first I thought it sounded like someone had fired a rifle at close range. I jumped up from bed to discover that a picture that had hung on my nephew's wall next to the bed for nearly 20 years had suddenly dropped to the ground with a resounding crack."

Looking for a logical explanation, Joan checked both the picture and the wall. "The nail was still in the wall and the wire on the back was still intact."

The next day, for scheduling reasons, not ghostly ones, the foursome headed for home. Joan conceded that although she was sorry to be leaving her sister and family again, she was definitely looking forward to getting home where there were no wandering souls to disturb her sleep.

Not surprisingly, Joan has given those supernatural incidents a great deal of thought over the years and wonders if the completely pristine land might somehow have contributed to the haunting. She expressed her thoughts this way: "As the land is unspoiled, save for cultivation of feed for the many head of cattle that roam about, perhaps then it is a natural conductor for things of a spiritual nature."

She may be correct. There is certainly no question that during her visits, forces we do not understand created an effective conduit for those from the other realm to visit our earthly one.

Harvey the Friendly Ghost

Opportunity, Montana, just northwest of Butte, is home to "Harvey the Friendly Ghost." About 10 years ago a man, whom we'll call Fred, and his young daughter moved into a house. At the time they were completely unaware that they'd be sharing their accommodation with someone from another realm.

Shortly after the two settled in, they began to hear strange sounds throughout the place. At first they just presumed that these were simply house noises and that once they became used to their new home they wouldn't be disturbed any longer. Until then, though, the father and daughter agreed that the sounds of people walking in empty parts of the house and slamming doors was pretty unnerving.

One evening, as Fred set the table for dinner, he was startled to watch as the spoons moved from where he'd put them. It was as if they were sliding from one side of the table to another—even though no one was touching them at the time. The forks and knives remained stationary. Amazed by what he was witnessing, the man called to his daughter to come see what was happening. Once she was standing beside her father, the man put the silverware back on the table. As the two people watched, the spoons moved again but as before, the knives and forks stayed where they'd been placed.

"Must be a slope in the table," they decided, well aware that their assumption was illogical.

The man's daughter always left the radio on as she slept at night. This routine of hers apparently did not please the ethereal being who was sharing the house with them because sometimes the volume on her radio would be turned down, and other times the radio would be turned off completely.

It wasn't until their dogs began barking at "nothing" that the pair knew that they were living in a haunted house. They named the spirit Harvey and proceeded to try to coexist with him. It wasn't easy. The presence had obviously been in the house longer than they had and was not pleased to have his own ghostly routine disturbed. For instance, Harvey apparently did not like it when the man left his reading glasses in a certain spot. Whenever the spectacles were left on one particular table, the man would find them somewhere else. Although that table was the most convenient place in the house for Fred to put his glasses when he wasn't wearing them, he did finally change his routine and adapt to the ghost's preference.

In all the time father and daughter lived in the house, Fred never once saw the ghost, but his daughter did. She described a thickening white mist that formed in her bedroom. As she watched, this fog began to take a definite shape. It was a child—a little blond boy to be specific. The girl watched in amazement as the boy's image became clear to her before, just as slowly, the vision vaporized. Seconds later waves formed in the girl's water bed.

No one ever saw Harvey again, but for the entire time they lived in that house, they were well aware of his ghostly presence.

Enduring Story

In 1892 the newspapers in Boise, Idaho, were filled with the story of a local haunting.

Jesse Black, a cigar-maker by trade, lived in a rented house on Eighth Avenue between State and Washington streets. His apprentice, a youngster named Daniel O'Brien, boarded with Jesse Black and his family. This arrangement had been in place for several years before a restless ghost upset the routine.

Late one Saturday night, after he'd been fast asleep for hours, Daniel awoke with the uncomfortable sensation that he was not alone in the room.

"Hello?" he called out in fright, but no one answered. Thinking that he'd just been dreaming and that he was alone, Daniel lay back down. Seconds later he sat bolt upright. The bedroom door was rattling and a chair that had been across the room was moving toward him. Poor Daniel was terrified, barely able to breathe. He thought of making a dash for the door, but before he could, a phantom voice spoke to him: "I've come from the other world, Daniel. You know me. We must speak."

Then, just as suddenly as it had arrived, the phantom intruder apparently left the premises. O'Brien lay awake for the rest of the night. In the morning he drew Mr. Black away from the others and explained what had occurred just a few hours before. Knowing that his apprentice was down-to-earth, reliable and not given to flights of fancy, the older man took young Daniel at his word and called in his trusted friend Albert Werner to help him investigate the source of the unnerving problem.

Werner planned to stay the night, sharing O'Brien's room. Everyone in the household retired early that evening, but no one was able to get much sleep because just a few hours later Daniel's screams of fright wakened everyone in the house. The spirit that had tried to contact him the night before was, apparently, not about to give up. This time the entity had written on Daniel's bedroom wall. Those words had not been penned by a normal writing instrument, though. This message had been scripted with light. Most frustratingly, no records exist of the content of that supernatural message.

As soon as he saw the words, Daniel relaxed a little bit. "It's my deceased sister's spirit trying to contact me," he announced to Werner and the Blacks, all of whom had assembled in his bedroom by that time. This conclusion may have calmed O'Brien, but it did nothing to quiet the fears of the others, for they were all sure that the entity occupying the room with them was a man.

Moments later they all heard rapping sounds coming from the walls. The same pattern of taps was sounded out on the wall over and over again. It seemed to be a code of some sort. There was no question that someone from another plane—Daniel was convinced that it was his sister—was trying frantically to get a message through to the living.

Terrified by their supernatural encounter, all the residents of the rented house moved out the next day. Uneasy rumors began to spread through Boise. O'Brien was a drinker, some said, and that's what caused his eerie experiences. Those closest to him, though, knew that Daniel O'Brien was a sober young man and they suspected that such talk was just an attempt by the upset townsfolk to quell their fears.

Days later a neighbor by the name of Beemer came forward to say that he was familiar with the house and had known for a long time that the place was haunted. Although he might have been trying to reassure people, this information succeeded only in making O'Brien more afraid because it would mean that a ghost other than the spirit of Daniel's beloved sister had been in the room with him.

This paranormal puzzle was never solved. Neither the Blacks nor their boarder ever went back to the haunted house, and Daniel was never bothered by ghosts again. To this day, no one knows for certain who or what caused the haunting, but this ghost story from Boise's early days has remained a local legend for all these years.

Resident Guardian

The next haunted house story takes place in Pueblo, Colorado. Longtime Pueblo resident Bob Campbell advises that the original settlement, a trading fort called El Pueblo, was abandoned after a Christmas Eve massacre in 1854. By 1860, however, people had begun to move back into the area. Many of the houses built during that resettlement period remain and now form the community of Historic South Pueblo. As the house this story revolves around was known to have been built in 1893, it is likely that it is located within that neighborhood.

We do not know exactly what year the Jackson family bought this property, but we do know that almost immediately after moving in, they were aware that there was something decidedly extraordinary about the place. At first the couple presumed that the noises they were hearing throughout their house at night were just noises that such an old house could be expected to make. They thought they would become accustomed to the sounds, even though Mrs. Jackson was often certain that an intruder from one dimension or the other was walking around in vacant parts of her new home. Before they'd had a chance to become comfortable with the sounds of the shuffling footsteps, something even stranger began to occur.

Both Mr. and Mrs. Jackson were devout Christians, and religious artifacts dotted many of the rooms in the big old house—at least these items were always there each evening. By morning, many of the crosses and pictures had often disappeared only to reappear—at random and from no apparent source—as the day wore on.

Given its rich history, it's no surprise that contemporary Pueblo, Colorado, is still the site of at least one infamous haunting.

Soon the Jacksons felt that there was no question they were sharing their home with a resident from the other side of time's curtain. They began to ask their neighbors if anyone had any information about the haunting or could suggest whose spirit might be in the house. Well, possibly someone could have but, as the couple soon found out, no one was willing to talk. Neighbors who had been friendly and welcoming at all other times were consistently unresponsive when either Mr. or Mrs. Jackson alluded to a possible ghost. One after another, people would either change the subject or terminate the conversation.

Meanwhile, the intensity of the haunting was increased. More than just religious items were missing. Coasters and other odd household objects would inexplicably disappear. Sometimes these small articles would reappear later. Others were never seen again.

To the best of their ability, the Jacksons began to adjust to living in their haunted old house. It wasn't until the ghost's image was actually seen—bending over their daughter's crib—that anything changed. Understandably, Mrs. Jackson gasped when she saw the apparition. It turned its ghostly face toward her and spoke. "Don't worry," the phantom said, "I'll take care of your daughter for you."

After that the Jacksons were reassured that the spirit in their house was a benign soul and not to be feared. And they were correct—their daughter grew up with a very special ghostly guardian watching over her. Despite determined attempts to discover the ghostly guardian's identity, they never did find out. For reasons that are still mysterious, not one of the Jacksons' neighbors would ever tell the couple anything about the history of the house.

Rats!

A certain building on Walnut Street in Genesee, Idaho, may have had quite a history! The ghost story took place in the mid-1970s. Not surprisingly, the full history of the haunting likely goes back years before that.

In 1974, women from three generations of one family—grandmother, mother and daughter—bought the Walnut Street house and began to settle in. When they heard strange noises echoing throughout their "new" home, they were not bothered. After all, the structure was old and they couldn't yet know what house noises it might routinely make.

But a few weeks later, when the grandmother was awakened from a deep sleep and saw an odd blue light glowing at the foot of her bed, she was not so dismissive. The poor woman sat bolt upright and stared at the strange sight before her eyes. It was a localized area of misty blue luminescence. Seconds later she became even more upset when she realized that the mysterious glow was becoming the size and shape of a human body. Paralyzed with fear, the woman could not do anything except continue to stare at the enigma. As she did, the grandmother was horrified to realize that the shape of a man was forming inside the glowing light. As she held her gaze, the manifestation became clearer and clearer.

She could see that the image was that of a tall, thin, elderly man and although she was still scared, the woman also noted that his look didn't seem threatening. Still, though, she was startled for a second time when the slightly transparent image spoke to her.

"Do you see me? Do you see me?" the ghost pleaded desperately before fading from sight in the blue glow. Then the blue mist itself vanished.

Understandably, the woman did not sleep again that night. The next day she made little of the incident to the family members who shared the home with her. She did not want to frighten them, perhaps unnecessarily.

Fully two weeks went by with nothing of a ghostly nature happening again. The three new occupants of the home had come to accept the frequent strange noises echoing from the rooms around them, deciding that the old place just made those noises. Even more reassuring was that there had been no more middle-of-the-night ghost sightings.

Sometime later the family invited a young friend from Australia to come to stay with them for a while. Their guest, a ballerina, was eager to see some American ballet. She was not anticipating having to share her bed with a ghost. When the spirit of a dark-haired woman pulled the girl's covers open and tried to get into the bed where the dancer had been sleeping peacefully, the girl screamed in terror. The image vanished, never to return.

After those instances, all was calm—right up to the day that the family watched in horror as an enormous silver-gray rodent scampered across their kitchen floor. That sight would have been unnerving enough, but as the rat was hugely oversized and completely transparent, it was even worse.

Several weeks later, a handyman came over to begin some renovations in the kitchen. He started by ripping up the existing floor. There, below the floorboards, was the mummified body of a long-dead rat. That could explain the appearance of the animal ghost but not either of the "human" supernatural appearances.

It is, of course, possible that the apparitions were just those of curious spirits floating by. It's also possible, though, that those ghosts had been in residence for many years and were responsible for all the apparently source-less noises the family continually heard.

Unfortunately, no records exist to update this story. If there have been further ghostly activities in the Walnut Street home, they have not been reported. Let's hope, for the mental and emotional well-being of the residents, that all is now calm in their home.

Old Fort Phantom

Great minds have advised us that we must learn from history. So many historical sites are haunted that you could say the spirits provide a lifelong education for some of us.

In the 1880s, Fort Sanders was an active military outpost. Today a residential area of Cheyenne, Wyoming, is located on the old fort site. The land's history is not completely gone—100 years later, a beautiful old stone house on Park Street has a spectral reminder of the fort.

The home is haunted by the ghost of a young cavalry officer. He is a pleasant spirit and has been happily accepted by the family now living in the house, who have named their visitor from the "other side" Luther. His image is completely formed, which makes him easily recognizable. It is obvious, witnesses report, that the ghost in this house is a revenant from the old fort. It is likely that he lost his life while stationed at the outpost. He's a young, thin man in a dark blue uniform.

Beyond startling people who've never seen him before, the ghost never frightens anyone. He is simply there, "living" in his time with those living in our time. The young man had a tragically short life but his afterlife has clearly been a long and hopefully satisfying time.

Rockies' Grey Lady

Through researching ghost stories over the past decade I have discovered that different cultures have different attitudes toward the existence of ghosts. The North American natives, for instance, take the existence of spirits and the spirit world for granted. For them such a reality simply and unequivocally exists.

In Japan the living memory of ancestors is revered.

In the British Isles ghosts are embraced and enjoyed. Often these spirits have become so much a part of the world that people have named them. Many of these ghosts must appear as misty female shadows, for an amazing number of the apparitions in the United Kingdom are referred to as "the Grey Lady" or "the Lady in Grey." Perhaps not surprisingly, traces of that heritage can be found in North America, with an occasional visit to the Rocky Mountain region.

The Grey Lady in the Rockies is thought to be the ghost of Catherine, an ancestor of an American pioneer

family, the Herondons. What makes her haunting especially interesting is that she came from England to the
U.S. nearly 350 years ago—as a ghost!

Over the years, her vaporous image has been seen by
different members of the Herondon family in different
parts of the country. Although the wraith keeps to a pre-
dictable schedule, Catherine's ghostly visits still manage to
scare her descendants, for she appears only to every second generation. Youngsters who have grown up hearing
tales of their ancient ancestor can be very skeptical—until
they are adults with their own children—children who see
this very recognizable ghost!

There is documentation to indicate that the spirit has
also appeared to her kin in Iowa and Texas. In the 1960s
the Lady in Grey made two appearances to one person in
two different houses—both in Laramie, Wyoming.
According to schedule, this reliable Lady should have
made at least one and perhaps two visits since then.

No one has ever speculated where the ghost goes when
she's not visiting the States. Of course, she could be
haunting relatives in England as one of their "grey ladies"
or perhaps she stays on to enjoy the Rocky Mountains. If
you see her floating about the rugged terrain you might
understandably be startled but there's no need to be
afraid. This "lady in grey" means no harm, nor is she a
portent of any ill fortune. She's merely a visitor from
beyond.

A Lingering Presence

Marie began to relate her family's ghost story by explaining that it took place in Hinton, an Alberta lumber town just east of the gates to Jasper National Park in the Canadian Rockies. She also explained, "We weren't believers until all of this started happening to us. We were just a plain 'ole' Canadian family."

The Berubes' ghost story began on Friday, March 1, 2002, when Sylvie, one of Marie's sisters, bundled her three daughters into the family car. She had some errands to do but had promised her little girls that first they could all enjoy a quick visit to Grandpa's house.

Marie explained that when the mother and three children arrived in front of the familiar house, Sylvie "sent her oldest girl to the door to see if Grandpa was there. It was snowing but there were no tracks anywhere in the snow."

They were sure their timing had been good because the lack of footprints in the snow indicated that no one had left the house in the past several hours. As well, the older man's truck was there, right beside the house. There was no question in Sylvie's mind that her father (commonly and fondly known as JP) was home. Sylvie's oldest daughter, Jennifer, jumped out of the car and made her way through the snow toward the door to her grandfather's house.

The child knocked at the door several times. Disappointingly, though, Grandpa didn't come to greet her.

"She came back to the car and told her mother there had been no answer. Sylvie asked her daughter if she had tried the door handle to see if the lock was off or on.

Jennifer said 'no' but offered to go back and try. From what I understand, my sister replied by saying, 'We don't have that much time anyway. Grandpa is probably sleeping so we'll just come back later.' "

And they did. The three girls and their mother drove to the business district in Hinton to tend to the chores that had taken them out of the house in the first place.

Meanwhile, Sylvie's husband, Chris, was also spending what he thought was a very ordinary Friday. As Marie explained, "My brother-in-law Chris was working away at his desk on this snowy Friday. It was around 3 PM. He was writing something so had his arms on the desk in front of him. He was alone in the room. Suddenly, someone grabbed the back of his arm and squeezed it several times."

The man was understandably startled by the sensation, especially as he knew he was alone in the room. Marie said, "Chris immediately looked around. There was no one in his office. As a matter of fact, no one was even remotely close to his work area."

Undoubtedly what had just happened made Chris feel unnerved but what he thought was especially strange, according to Marie, "was as soon as this happened, he thought of my father. He called Dad at his house, but there was no answer."

Objectively, Chris really had no reason to be overly concerned about JP or the fact that the man didn't answer the phone. There could have been dozens of perfectly reasonable, and happy, explanations for that. But Chris simply could not accept what his sixth sense was trying to tell him. Mentally and emotionally the younger man felt uncomfortable, and the discomfort all seemed to revolve around JP's well-being.

Over the next two hours Chris made that same call several times. Much to his distress, each call had the same result—JP did not answer the phone.

Later that afternoon when Chris had arrived home after work, he told Sylvie about the strange incident of feeling his arm being squeezed when no one was near him and that starting at that very strange moment, he'd suddenly felt very concerned about Sylvie's father.

When Sylvie said that she also hadn't seen her dad, their worry increased. Marie couldn't help thinking that the pristine condition of the freshly fallen snow was an important indicator that all was not well.

She said, "We knew that no one had been in or out of Dad's house for quite a while because there would've been tracks from his feet and the truck's tires in the snow. Whenever there was a snowfall Dad would go out and shovel right away and also brush off his truck. This hadn't been done. Something wasn't right."

Still, not wanting to panic unnecessarily, the pair prepared dinner for their three daughters and sat down to eat their meal as a family. Neither Chris nor Sylvie, though, was going to be able to enjoy the evening until they knew for certain that her father was all right.

Marie related what happened next. "At about 8:30 PM, Chris decided to go over to my dad's house in case he was sick or needed help in any way. After all, Dad was 67 years old. Something could have happened.

"Chris walked into the house. It hadn't been locked. He found my dad on the loveseat in the living room. Dead.

Dad had died of a massive heart attack. The coroners couldn't tell us how long his body might have lain there. Their educated guess was 'anywhere from 12 to 48 hours.' "

Marie continued, "This meant that when Jennifer went to his door her Grandpa was already dead. If she had tried the door handle, as she was ready to go back and do, the door would have opened. That little girl, 10 years of age, would have been the one to have found him."

As anyone who's ever been through the death of a close family member knows, there is a great deal to handle at a time when no one feels like handling anything extra at all.

Marie and Sylvie's first task was to notify their siblings in Ontario. This is never a pleasant job, but for the Berube family it was made even more onerous by the large size of the family.

"We were all very upset, emotions were running high as we were trying to reach our brothers and sisters. Sylvie and I began to plan Dad's funeral."

In order to get closure on the relationship she'd had with her father, Marie needed to see her father's body. "We went to the morgue. I really felt as though I wanted to see my dad. As I was standing there looking at him I felt peace because it didn't seem like it was Dad lying there but merely a shell that was once just his body. It didn't feel like that was or had been my dad. My sister and I talked with him briefly and said our good-byes. Then we went back to my sister's house."

As some of the family began to assemble, their beloved father's body was taken east to Edmonton to have an autopsy performed. It had been a sudden and unexpected death, so for legal and medical reasons an official cause of death had to be determined.

Marie continued, "That evening we sat in my sister's living room talking and, of course, crying. The phone rang. It was my niece from North Bay, Ontario, calling. I went into the kitchen and took the call in there. She had just heard the news about dad and was really upset. She wanted to know the details of what had happened."

Marie explained the circumstances to her niece as best she could and added that at this point their biggest concern was whether their father had suffered before he died. Marie personally felt very bad because, as she put it, she "hadn't talked to Dad in a while…I had never got a chance to tell him how much I loved him. My niece and I began to talk about this on the phone. I was standing in front of the window looking outside and crying. The snow had stopped. Everything outside was calm. All of a sudden I felt something very warm huddle around me and brush up against the back of my pant leg. I looked up into the reflection in the window and there was a definite shadow behind me—a shadow that was a little taller than I am. It was a dark outline of a person. You could clearly see the shape of the head and shoulders but could not see the face or any other details in the reflection in the window. It felt like someone was giving me a hug. I thought maybe my sister or Chris had come in to give me a hug, but when I turned back, there was no one there."

Marie said, "I freaked out. I called my sister into the room to tell her what had happened. I was so distraught that I had let go of the phone. It wasn't that I was scared, it was just a really weird feeling, especially when no one was there. My sister tried to calm me down and told me I should talk to Chris about what had just happened. She proceeded to tell me what had happened to him at work the afternoon that Dad had passed away. I hadn't known about Chris' experience until this had happened."

Marie's knees buckled and she sat down. "I was really shaken up. I did tell Chris what had happened. His face dropped. He went into the living room and stood in the same exact spot in front of the window that I had been standing at when I saw the strange shadow. The weather was still calm with no wind whatsoever."

Standing at the window, Chris spoke. He said, "Okay, JP, show me a sign that it is you."

Marie continued, "As soon as Chris said this, one single huge gust of snow blew past the window. That gave Chris one big chill, I'll tell you."

It soon became apparent that the mourning family's strange encounters were just beginning.

Marie recalled, "The next day, we told my brother Claude, my sister Suzanne and Yvan, one of my nephews, what had happened the previous evening. That's when another sister piped up. She told us that at about 5:00 in the morning of the day Dad's body was found, she was wakened by a very strange dream. Dad showed up in her dream with his first wife, Suzanne's mother, who had passed away a year before."

Marie recounted her sister's experience. "She saw Dad coming to her. At first she thought it was a just a dream. Considering, though, that he did die sometime around then, we wonder now if maybe that was the moment when our dad passed from his physical body."

The first night they were gathered, Marie did not sleep well. "My daughter came and crawled into bed with me in the wee hours of the night. She said that she'd seen her grandpa coming down the hall. I looked out my room into the hall, and there was nothing that I could see."

But the ghost of Marie's father was still in the house.

"The next night my niece Jennifer complained of the same thing. What made this especially eerie was that the kids hadn't talked to each other about the encounter. That night my sister was getting ready to go to bed. Moments later, she came out of her room as white as a ghost claiming that while she'd been alone in the room someone or something had pinched her."

There was no doubt in any of the relatives' minds exactly what was happening. "When we were kids, if Dad was upset with us he would grab the back of our arm, exactly the way Chris had been grabbed that day. The really odd thing is, though, that Chris had never known that Dad used to do this. Also, when we were kids, Dad would pinch us lightly when we were playing around. He's always say it was a mosquito or something. Dad always liked to joke around."

At first the sisters and one of the brothers tried to dismiss these strange occurrences. "We thought maybe we were just missing Dad and so our imagination was playing tricks on us."

And according to Marie, this is the attitude they tried to carry on with. "After the funeral we went to Dad's house to separate his belongings. We'd agreed that each of us would take a little something to remember Dad by. Just going into the place where my dad had died was eerie in itself. But to make matters worse, things we couldn't explain happened in there as well. For instance, Dad's best friend, Darlene, had come with us. She was the executor of his will. Darlene was standing in the kitchen of Dad's home and all of a sudden got a very cold breeze against her. This was especially weird because Dad always kept his place so warm. The furnace was always going."

Despite the warmth in the house that morning, Darlene felt a sudden and frigid draft blow up against her when there was no physical way that could have happened. The evidence was certainly piling up, but, perhaps in an attempt to stay calm, the family members tried to keep their heads about them.

Marie admitted that "it felt a little weird but we didn't think much more about it."

When the group finished what they'd gone to the house to do, they left, but Darlene stayed on to attend to more work. Sometime later the woman finished her chores, locked the house and prepared to go back to her own home.

"As she was backing out of Dad's driveway, Darlene happened to glance at the kitchen window. She saw the window coverings open. Then she saw a man who bore an eerie resemblance to my dad. He was looking out the kitchen window."

At that point Marie added the kicker: "My Dad always did this when he heard someone come up the driveway."

Darlene was concerned and went back into the house. Initially she was afraid that a member of the family had been left behind in the house. "She went in and did a thorough search of the house. No one was in there. No one she could see, that is."

The next day, JP's body was cremated. After the funeral each of the brothers and sisters took home some of their father's ashes. Perhaps this is part of the reason JP's spirit has lingered as a haunting presence in their lives.

"We still have a lot of things happening. The most common one is that as soon as I come into my house, or my sister goes into her house, we get a brief whiff of our dad's distinctive scent. It's as if he is still greeting us at the door, like he used to do at his place when he was alive."

Marie acknowledged that they were uncomfortable with this phenomenon at first but by now they are well used to it and even look forward to their father's greeting from the other side.

"Now when we enter our houses we say, 'Hi Dad! Hope you had a good day.' "

But it isn't just the sisters in the Rocky Mountain foothills town of Hinton who experience their father's spirit. Every one of the deceased man's children, even those living thousands of miles from his former home, have regular encounters with the man's ghost.

In October 2002, seven months after her father's death, Marie had an eerily vivid dream. She described it this way: "My dad came to me and put his hand on my shoulder. He told me that he was all right, that he hadn't suffered and that I had no need to worry."

The woman continued, "I was crying really hard in my dream. He said he loved me and that he would always be watching out for 'His Girls.' I think that meant my sister and me as well as our four daughters. When I woke up from this dream I had felt like I had actually talked to my dad. My pillow was just soaked with tears."

Marie continued, "A few nights later I was having trouble getting to sleep. My daughter was sleeping beside me and I was trying hard to go to sleep but hadn't been able to. I had been lying with my back toward the door for quite a while when I felt as though someone was watching me. I turned toward the door and saw a bright shining light."

After a minute or so the illumination extinguished itself but was replaced by another sensory hint. "I could smell my dad again," Marie attested.

This ghost story apparently continues—even as I write about it. JP's manifestation remains most welcome in any of his children's homes.

"Maybe Dad is watching over us, protecting us in a sense, making sure we are all right. We have all come to realize that Dad may have passed over to the other side but he still seems to come back every now and then to check on us and show us that his joking nature has not changed."

One example of the ghost still joking with them is that a particular picture in Sylvie's living room shakes and then suddenly falls off the wall quite regularly now. It never did that before.

Marie also noted that "once when Sylvie was alone in the house she lay down for a nap. As she started to drift off to sleep she felt someone rubbing her tummy. She thought it was her husband but when she opened her eyes there was no one there."

Supporting the theory that animals are more receptive to beings from beyond than we are, Marie advised that "when we feel my dad's presence in the house or smell his scent, my daughter's hamster, Spots, acts as though he is watching someone. I don't know if the animal can sense or see someone in my living room, but Spots will watch and stare at something for quite a long time. Also, when I turn off the television set, it often turns right back on. This happens as much as five times in one night. If it gets annoying I just say 'Dad, that's enough. The game is over now' and it stops. It is almost as though I can see him sitting in the easy chair laughing, thinking it is funny. He was a practical joker in life and used to do things like that. I don't actually see his image but it's as though I do."

Perhaps when JP's presence has finally had his fill of protecting and joking around with his kids, his spirit might enjoy a journey to the nearby Rocky Mountains and the gorgeous geography of Jasper National Park.

2
Highways
and
Byways

From hiking trails to highways, rivers, streams and lakes, getting around the grand obstacles of the Rocky Mountains has always posed challenges. And not all of those challenges are of this world.

Cleanup Crews from the Past

On a beautiful, early summer's evening in the mid-1980s, Susan was doing what thousands of her peers all over the continent were doing—driving to her summer job. Sue had always been good with kids, so she was studying to become a teacher. As she was also something of a jock, she was delighted to have been offered the opportunity to coach at a high school basketball camp. Susan had packed her car in anticipation of what she imagined would be a scenic and straightforward trip from her home in Lethbridge, Alberta, to her destination in the south of British Columbia. The road conditions were perfect and before long she could see the silhouette of the Rocky Mountain peaks.

The Crowsnest Pass area in southwestern Alberta consists of a string of little towns huddled in the mountain valleys near the border between Canada and the United States. In the 1800s and early 1900s, these communities were busy coal-mining centers. Like most Albertans, Susan knew the area's history. She'd certainly heard about the Frank Slide. The town of Frank is nestled at the foot of Turtle Mountain. In the early hours of April 29, 1903, an avalanche of boulders crashed down from that mountain's face, burying and demolishing everything in its path—including the sleeping town of Frank and most of its residents.

No one can ever know exactly how many lives were lost in that disaster because Frank, as with all the towns along the coal-mining corridor, was a boomtown. Because many of the residents were transient workers living in

Ghosts return to the Frank Slide in Alberta, where giant slabs of broken rock bear testament to nature's awesome power.

makeshift structures and following the mining jobs from one town to another, it was impossible to know precisely what the town's population was when the tons of gigantic rocks slid down the mountainside. Even today, those enormous boulders remain strewn across the landscape, permanent reminders of nature's deadly power.

Over the 100 years since the slide, many people have reported seeing ghostly shapes and shadows hovering about the enormous rocks that were tossed down at the mountain's will. Some people have seen even more. A colleague of Susan's, whose family lived in the Crowsnest Pass, told me that still, every summer, anomalies occur when tourists who've stopped to take photographs at this strange and ominous location get a supernatural surprise. When they get their films developed, they find extra images on the one or two photos they've taken. Invariably, these images form an outline—an outline of a person who wasn't there (they thought!) when the picture had been posed for and taken.

Whether or not you have seen a hovering manifestation before your eyes or have captured a ghostly manifestation on film, it is impossible to drive by the site of the Frank Slide without being in awe of it. And on that clear and warm summer's evening, Susan was no exception. Her thoughts must have been only fleeting, though, because as she drove along the curvy and hilly highway through the Crowsnest Pass, she suddenly became aware that a very large truck was following her, and following far too closely for Susan to feel comfortable. Each time she'd reach the peak of one of the highway hills and then drive back down the other side, she hoped that she had shaken the huge, dangerous tailgating truck riding her car's rear bumper.

But she hadn't.

Every time she reached level ground, the lights of the truck were there again, shining in her rearview mirror and lighting up the interior of her car. The two vehicles descended yet another hill. The truck was still right behind her. Though she wasn't easily frightened, Susan was concerned. It almost seemed that the driver was pursuing her, that the truck was actually gaining speed steadily. It was so close behind her car that Susan couldn't see its bumper in her mirror. Worse, when she turned to look behind her, all she could see was the monstrous vehicle's grill.

Susan stepped down harder on the gas pedal in an attempt to put more highway between her and the aggressive truck driver behind her. As she ascended the next hill she realized that she had succeeded in increasing the distance between the two vehicles—but only slightly. Taking a deep breath, she told herself, *That idiot driving the truck will never catch up again now.*

But he did.

Susan recalled, "It was like the truck driver was looking *over* my car, beyond it, as though he wasn't even aware that I was on the road. If I slowed down, the truck slowed down. If I sped up, it sped up. I was hoping the truck would pass me but it didn't."

Someone or something had to end this road game that Susan had no interest in playing.

"I was so nervous about this truck being behind me and then disappearing from view that I was preoccupied with what was behind me rather than what was in front," Susan explained before adding, "then, as I pulled away from the truck and went over a rise, the other vehicle just ceased to exist. It did not come down over the rise with me."

Susan may have hoped her bizarre encounter was over, but she wouldn't have put money on it. "I wasn't convinced at that time that I had shaken the truck. I was still checking in the rearview mirror looking for it but at that point, it seemed the truck simply ceased to exist."

A woman named Susan was eyewitness to some bizarre events near the slide site.

Susan was in for another surprise when, as she explained, "less than a minute after 'losing' the truck, I noticed lights ahead of me."

There, just a few feet in front of her, were people, dozens and dozens of people, standing near the road. Stranger still, instead of the truck's headlights illuminating the interior of Susan's car, it was the surrounding area that was illuminated. It was nearly midnight but as bright as day outside.

Susan slowed her car down to less than 10 miles (16 kilometers) an hour. She took time to look around her.

She could hardly believe the scene she was traveling through. Not only were there more than 100 people along the road working at various tasks, but there were also many pieces of heavy equipment on and beside the road. The machines looked like earth-movers or road-building equipment of some sort.

Fascinated, Susan recalls that she "rolled opened the car window. I thought there might be a flag person giving directions or something. The whole area was completely lit up. It was as bright as day there. I drove directly past the flagman. He was close enough to the car that he could have touched it. I even remember looking into his eyes for a short time. He didn't look at all threatening."

Seconds later, Susan noticed another strange thing: utter and complete silence. She could see hundreds of people working with the heavy pieces of equipment, yet, even with her car window down, Susan could not hear any sound at all.

"This 'work site' was very active and very well-lit. There were quite a few machines moving in the area and numerous people. The activity was primarily to my left, but at this point in time I was very spooked and my focus was shifting from the road to the site to my rearview mirror. Even after I passed the site I could still see the lights from it in my rearview mirror as I continued to travel. I drove through the area without incident. The time from losing sight of the truck in my rearview mirror to passing the 'work site' couldn't have been much more than a minute or so."

Later, Susan remembered thinking, *This whole scene seems to be from another time.*

After a stretch of less than half a mile, the apparitions of people and the manifestations of road-building equipment receded into the background. Susan realized with relief that the truck was no longer behind her. She also realized something else very peculiar. The eerily silent machines she had seen moving rocks from the road were not yellow, as was all the road-building equipment Susan had ever seen before. These machines were green.

Sometime later the explanation for that color difference registered in Susan's mind. Those pieces of road-building equipment, the big truck following her so dangerously, as well as the workers she had seen on the road and operating the machines, were not of her time.

Driving through the mountains on her way to coach at a basketball camp in southern British Columbia, Susan had driven through the curtain of time. She had experienced retrocognition—seeing a place as it had existed in the past. What she had seen was a permanent haunting—spirits from the past forever reliving an event that must have taken place immediately after the side of Turtle Mountain had crashed down—April 1903.

The trauma of the enormous tragedy that was the Frank Slide scarred the psychic landscape in that part of the Crowsnest Pass to such a degree that its aural imprint had become imbedded in the very atmosphere of the area—only to be played back over and over again—into eternity.

This supernatural phenomenon is not common, but, as you have just read, it does occur. That summer night in the mid-1980s, while driving through mountainous terrain, Susan encountered an extremely dramatic display of the long-dead past being replayed before a "live" audience.

Encounter Denied

The following paraphrase of one man's 1889 story of his ghostly encounter shows just how close some people come to a spooky encounter—when they least expect it.

It was a hot, sunny morning in mid-August—August 12, to be precise—when we set out on our hike. The purpose of the trek was to collect rock specimens for W.C. Hart, a geologist whom I greatly admired. He had hired Joe Shepier as a mountain guide, while my friend Richard and I were to act as assistants on the expedition. Our destination that day was Cameron Pass on the Cache de la Poudre River in north-central Colorado.

At first it seemed to be a reasonably undemanding journey. So it was strange that we were never able to complete our day's mission. Stranger still was that, until the day they died, neither Hart nor Shepier ever once admitted to having had a moment's discomfort during the trip. As their opinions were the ones that counted, theirs became the accepted rendition of the events. Richard and I, however, were wont to tell a very different tale.

It's difficult to remember now exactly which came first—did Richard become unnerved or had circumstances already turned a little weird by the time he became anxious? Such specifics don't really matter by now, I suppose, but I do recall clearly that our initial joviality, borne of fresh energy reserves, eager anticipation and a sense of adventure, had worn off as we trudged silently along the rocky terrain of Cameron Pass. Looks of sheer, grim determination had replaced our enthusiastic moods.

It was just less than half an hour after that when I noticed that Richard's pace had slowed considerably. Gradually slowing the rate of my own footsteps, I hung back a bit from Hart and Shepier to wait for my colleague to catch up. As Richard came nearer I could see a distinctly strained look on his face, so I called out some encouraging words to him.

He replied immediately in a strained voice, "What is it about this place? It makes me feel uneasy. There's a desolate weirdness abounding here and I don't like the feeling it gives."

Just then Shepier and Hart noticed that we had fallen some distance behind them.

"Ahoy there, my men." Hart called out. "I didn't pay a day's wages to have you merely stroll along behind. Shake a leg. Catch up. Besides, if you don't, you'll miss some fun. Shepier was just spinning a yarn. You'll want to hear the tale, I'm sure. He said this place is haunted—haunted by the Spirit of Cameron Pass."

Just at that moment, a shudder, almost a convulsion, ran through my body. I stood stock-still and looked around. The land formations suddenly looked very strange to me—foreboding somehow. The air around us had become still and cold. I cast my eyes over to Richard. He stared back at me with a vacant look in his eyes. At that moment he seemed less like a human being and more like a statue, completely immobile. When he finally spoke it was more like a stammer.

"It's dark. Why is it so dark all of a sudden?" he asked.

Up ahead, Hart and Shepier chuckled. Hart pointed back at us. My admiration for Hart was growing thin.

How very rude he and Shepier were. They actually seemed to be enjoying our obvious discomfort.

"Gather 'round. We'll stop here for a rest and I'll tell you the tale of the Spirit of Cameron Pass," Shepier called out to us before adding the eerie promise "It'll curdle your blood."

I gave a small nod of agreement and began to make my way toward them. I'd gone only a few steps when Richard, some 10 feet [3 meters] behind me, gave a sharp cry.

"What is that?" he yelled as he looked at the ground beside his left foot.

"Come along," I urged, for I could see that it was the disemboweled body of a hare. There was no point in his standing and staring at the animal's corpse. Hart and Shepier had already set up a temporary stopping place at a crook in the trail. Shepier had already begun to tell the tale that none of us asked to hear.

"Yes, boys, there's a ghost here. They call her the Spirit of Cameron Pass. I've seen her many times myself. She's said to be the soul of an emigrant's daughter. The poor girl had been driven from camp by her enraged father because she loved a man. Her father did not approve. He thought she loved not wisely but too well."

Richard's face was ashen, and I have to admit that I was not particularly happy to be told we were in close proximity to a restless spirit.

The mountaineer continued, "Her spirit is a thief. She frequently stole food and even equipment from the camps of any hunters who ventured within the precincts of this area, her uninviting domain."

For a moment we were all silent, sipping cold tea from tin cans and pondering the possibility of ghosts—this one in particular. We all knew Shepier's reputation. It was widely acknowledged that he was a man of great courage. As he spoke so matter-of-factly about this eerie situation, I decided that his bravery exceeded mine. Suddenly he looked up past Richard and me. He stared in silence for a minute. When he did speak it was to utter words that I shall remember all my life.

"The Spirit of Cameron Pass is approaching," he said in a low voice as he pointed to a spot just behind Richard and me.

I was frightened to look but more frightened not to look. There, just feet from where I sat, was a strange being, the likes of which I'd never seen before. The manifestation was moving swiftly toward our little camp. She came within yards of us before stooping to pick up a large stone. At that second I felt that the rest of my life could have been measured in seconds. I was sure that this apparition was going to hurl the rock directly at my head, but after staring at us for a moment she cradled the stone to her body and ran away. Seconds later the ghost, and the rock, had vanished.

"Come on, men," Shepier called as he bolted in the direction she had been running. He had his rifle under his right arm, which, even at the time, struck me as ridiculous. What possible protection could a bullet offer against an ethereal being?

Richard and I stayed where we were, content to watch this supernatural encounter from what we hoped was a safe distance. We waited there for over an hour before the other two returned. When they did they looked distraught and seemed flustered.

Hart stated with mock conviction that they had caught up to the phantom. He explained, "The creature dropped the rock and sped onward to the opening of a cave. We followed behind and seconds later we discovered the still warm body of a dead woman. The fright of seeing us and the exertion of running from us had killed her."

He continued, "There's no need for either of you to see the corpse. It's a grisly sight. She was perhaps 25 years of age. Her clothing was strange. Not like anything I'd ever seen before. That must've been what had made everyone who'd seen her over the years think that she was a ghost. We gave her a decent burial before we left."

No one said anything for a time. It was likely clear to Shepier and Hart that neither Richard nor I believed their tale, and the veracity was not confirmed when Hart announced emphatically that, even though we had not yet picked up even one rock formation for his collection, it was time to head home.

Hart and Shepier told their version of their encounter with the Spirit of Cameron Pass to anyone who would listen. Soon it became accepted, but incorrect, knowledge that the image people had long thought was a ghost had, in fact, been a wild woman scavenging for food.

To my knowledge, Richard has never said a word to anyone about his adventure on that strange day in August. And I, only now, today, nearly seven years after the fact, feel comfortable enough to speak of that day when I know for certain I saw a ghost—the ghost who haunted Cameron Pass.

Sadly, the name of this one man, the only one of the four honest enough to relate the incident as it actually was—a ghost story—was not revealed in the article which ran in several North American newspapers dated June 12, 1889.

(Almost) Living History

Is there a difference between encountering a ghost and being in a haunted place? Apparently there is. Some areas, it seems, have been permanently affected (haunted, that is) by events that have occurred there, and phantom sights, sounds and even smells remain for years after the incident.

Excellent examples of this phenomenon are the psychic reverberations that still echo through the battlefield at Little Bighorn (see my *Ghost Stories of the Rocky Mountains*, Lone Pine Publishing, 1999). Such traumatic instances can somehow become imprinted in a place's atmosphere and then are continually replayed as though on an infinite supernatural loop. If you observe an area that has been scarred in this way you are not so much seeing ghosts as experiencing retrocognition—sensing the place as it was years before.

There is reported to be just such a haunted place in Golden Spike National Park on the north shores of the Great Salt Lake in Utah. This is where, amid pomp and circumstance, the last spike—a golden one—was driven on May 10, 1869, to complete the ribbon of steel across the United States of America.

The undertaking had been mammoth—in size and in importance. Special infantrymen protected not only the project but also the thousands of workers laboring to complete it. The exhausted workers had all quickly abandoned the camps where they'd lived during the arduous undertaking. There was no point in staying, for the job was finished. It was time to move on to another project.

According to the witnesses who have experienced retrocognition at that spot, not every aspect of those pioneer workers left at the same time. People out enjoying a day in the park have reported hearing voices involved in intense conversation even though there is no one else for miles around. Others have heard and seen a phantom train traveling along on train tracks—train tracks that have not existed for decades.

Before those tracks were torn up, train engineers used to exchange hair-raising stories about watching in horror as another train—one that should not have been there—approached theirs on the same track. These terrified engineers would try desperately to bring their train to a stop and thereby lessen the severity of the inevitable collision. Each time, though, just at the instant when the two trains should have hit, the other locomotive had disappeared—vanished completely.

The best-documented incident of retrocognition at the park occurred in 1979 when a group of friends who were interested in history assembled at the ominously haunted place to reenact the march made by military guards just before completion of the transcontinental rail line. The point of any historical reenactment is to let people get as close to experiencing the original event as they possibly can. What happened to a man named Steve Ellison during the contrived adventure meant that he likely came as close to experiencing living history as possible.

Ellison had been assigned a watch shift that would run through the middle of the night. To keep from succumbing to boredom, he spent the first part of his shift roaming around the site. He knew the area well, and the night was beautiful, so the man was thoroughly enjoying being where he was.

Then, for no reason he could identify, Steve Ellison began to feel somewhat unsettled. He stood up and looked around but could see nothing out of the ordinary—nothing, that is, except a small ball of light in the distance. The glowing orb was swinging from side to side as though someone was walking toward the camp carrying a lantern.

As the strange little light faded from his sight, Steve began to relax. Seconds later, however, he was jarred by another enigmatic occurrence. He heard the distinctive chugging noise of an approaching train. He knew he couldn't discount those sounds because they were so easily recognizable and he well knew that there were no longer train tracks nearby.

As he stood paralyzed with fear, the chugging continued toward him and then past him. The sounds were accompanied by a localized rush of air. When he was able to move, Steve made his way back to the camp and the security of his fellow history buffs. He sat there until he had collected himself and then headed back to where he'd heard and seen the supernatural sights. The phantom train had gone, but the air was filled with the muffled sounds of many conversations taking place at one time.

It was at that moment that Steve Ellison realized the voices he was hearing had spoken in exactly that area—

more than 100 years before. He was hearing the echoes from the past. Slowly relaxing into the retrocognition he was encountering, the man also realized that he could feel the long-dead workers moving about as they accomplished their tasks.

Although Ellison was no longer frightened, he was definitely unnerved and for no reason he was able to understand, he suddenly felt tremendously sad. Somehow the overwhelming fatigue that the workers felt as they labored had been stored in the area's atmosphere.

Thankfully for lovers of true ghost stories, Steve Ellison went public with his experiences that night. He even candidly admitted that he had been so affected by his paranormal encounter that for some time after he made a point to pray for the souls that he felt had been trapped on this side of the curtain of time. Perhaps his prayers were answered and the restless spirits have gone on to their final, and peaceful, reward.

Ancient Equine Apparition

Sometime in the 1880s, just four hours after Friday, October 30, became Saturday, October 31, Charles Penrose and a man we shall call Jones boarded the Utah and Northern narrow gauge train at Butte, Montana. They were headed for a day's fishing near the Great Divide—a place where, according to a newspaper article of the time, "one may ride through a blinding snow storm on the 4th of July and, when those snows melt at midday, little streams trickle down the Divide, flowing east to the Atlantic Ocean and west to the Pacific Ocean."

As they rode, the two men looked forward to their day-long escape from routine. A "profusion of blue and white flowers" alongside the train tracks was a refreshing sight for their city-sore eyes. Jones later recalled that the train had made its way "south through a canyon and past Forest's ranch before continuing on for 30 miles [48 kilometers] along the bed of Silver Bow Creek's worked-out placer diggings. The coarse gravel and clay were washed bare and brown. Limestone glistened in the morning sun. Teal ducks were resting in a stream."

This was clearly an idyllic place.

As the engine pulled the rolling stock "over the summit tower beyond the timber line it was 10 AM. We got off the train and arranged to be picked up there again and taken back to Butte later in the day. The natural green carpet beneath our feet was sprinkled with pretty tiny wild-flowers."

Grateful for the peace and beauty of their surroundings, the pair headed toward Big Hole River, "a swift stream some 40 feet [12 meters] wide" where they would spend several hours fishing.

"By 6 PM it was twilight. Our fish baskets were full and our fly hooks were empty. The weight of our loaded creel and fowling-pieces strapped over our shoulders rapidly became oppressive after a day's arduous sport."

By the time they reached the spot where the train was to come pick them up, the men were tired. It was just after dark when they heard the sounds of a train approaching. Oddly, the locomotive did not seem to be slowing. Jones and Penrose waved madly to signal someone on board, but the train rumbled right past them. Seconds later the train was gone and the two men were left stranded in the wilderness.

Figuring they had no other choice, the pair began the impossibly long walk back to Butte. On and on they trudged, their feet and backs sore from the weight of their heavy loads. They had gone some distance before Penrose realized that he could not walk another step. There was no question but that the men would have to spend the night exactly where they were. After setting up a rough camp-site, Penrose and Jones made themselves a tasty dinner of their day's catches.

Moments after they'd finished the last mouthful, "suddenly there appeared to the left and perhaps a hundred yards in front, a light. It looked to be a lantern held in a man's hand. We let out a joyful shout to greet this welcome sight. We both called to the image repeatedly. The light moved steadily along, about 3 feet [1 meter] above the ground, with a consistent, yellow radiance. It moved out farther and then shot high into the air, fell to the

surface with a slight crackling sound and went out like a
flash. Our amazement was beyond words. We turned to
look at each other. What we saw curdled our blood. That
yellowish haze seemed to have become luminous. All over
the valley faint, phosphorescent patches of light hovered
over the mounds and in the sedgy hollows. A cold breath,
a wind from some narrow intersecting gorge, swept into
the valley and the lights went out. The darkness was even
denser than before."

Jones continued, "Some 150 yards [140 meters]
away there swept into view a great, glaring light, for all
the world like the headlight of a locomotive. With a
distinctly audible whizz, a steady whirr and a dazzling
radiance, this light rushed towards us. With a cry of
horror, we sprang out of its apparent line of motion,
first to one side and then to the other. This glow rushed
within 10 feet [3 meters] of us and then went out, once
more leaving the darkness blacker. All over the sullen
surface of the marsh, the dim patches of the light
became visible. Every mound of earth seemed to nour-
ish a flame, pale and evanescent, yet sometimes clear
enough to define the outline of the surface. The entire
atmosphere became semi-luminous."

The men stood and watched, paralyzed with fear.

"There appeared a gigantic mass of whitish flame,
which moved with inconceivable quickness. Then it
stayed on one tree for more than half an hour. The
vaporous mass whose strange antics were almost incredi-
ble soon took on a superficial resemblance to the outline
of a horse. It would suddenly shoot high into the air with
a clear blue effulgence before descending to the earth and

flitting along the ridge for several hundred yards [about 500 meters], returning at last to rest on the tree.

"Hundreds of other lesser and hazier white lights now seemed crawling all over the valley. Phosphorescent luminous vapor, sometimes in some fantastic shape but generally formless, appeared on every mound."

This supernatural light show was an endurance test for the men's nerves. "For something less than two hours this continued. Often a great horse-like flame appeared clearly. It never disappeared totally from the right-hand ridge."

Slowly, the men were beginning to gain some control over the fear that had them frozen. They began to move away from the paranormal activity. "As we had moved at least 8 miles [13 kilometers] in this time, it suddenly occurred to us that this equine apparition must have moved along the boundary range of the valley with a progress about as rapid as our own."

The luminescent beast was following them.

"Several of the mound lights were always between our standpoint at any given time and the point on the crest of the ridge where the big light appeared. At last the bounding ranges of the hills drew nearer together, the low mounds seemed to have disappeared and our path again became a narrow strip of firm ground at the foot of canyon walls. A brisk breeze blew from the northeast and cleared away the fog. After an hour's walk we were in the valley of Silver Bow Creek, near Forest's ranch."

They ran to the safety of the ranch house.

"Forest's hospitable hearth and the comforts of this once-famous stage station soon banished disagreeable memories of an adventure which, it became more and more apparent, would be hardly credible," Jones wrote some months later. "I had kept account of 67 distinct lights. We had never heard the old timers ever speak of anything like what we had just experienced and concluded that saying little or nothing about the strange encounter was best."

After a few hours' sleep, the pair prepared for the last leg of their long journey home. "As we left Forest's ranch the next morning, Big Ike Forest said with a laugh, 'Yer ain't seen nothin' of Old Bill yesterday? He went down the canyon in the mornin' to smoke a pipe on Chief Big Horse's grave over behind the range there, some 30 miles [48 kilometers] from here. Yesterday was Halloween, you know.'"

Without realizing it Charles Penrose and Edward Jones had happened across an enchanted place, where a spiritual man from a previous era was calling out to souls on Halloween—a time when the veil between this side of time and the other is said to be the thinnest.

But, how can we know that such an event ever took place? The answer can be found on the pages of any one of dozens of North American newspapers—the ones that were published in late March 1885!

A Wyoming Wonder

Ghost stories—and the people who read them—are all very different from one another. By definition, though, there is the one common theme of the ghost. One similarity, held up to all the differences, makes it very difficult to create an accurate or even widely accepted definition for the word "ghost."

To further confuse matters, some stories, such as the one that follows, manage to muddy the waters even more.

By the winter of 1946, World War II was finally last year's history. The soldiers, "our boys" who had lived to tell of the horrors, were home again. Both the formal and informal celebrations of the war's end had been held. All over the world it was time for everyone, especially the soldiers, to settle back into being at home and at peace and to begin picking up pieces of lives deserted years before.

Gordon Barrow was just one of those former soldiers. Like all those who'd returned, he was mightily relieved to be able to put the misadventures of military life behind him. Little did Barrow know that he would soon experience an eerie supernatural adventure.

After resting at his parents' home for some time, Gordon realized he was ready to consider his future. Being a clever and ambitious young man, he enrolled at the University of Wyoming in Laramie.

One weekend, in the icy cold heart of a treacherous Wyoming winter, Barrow drove the 100 miles (161 kilometers) from school in Laramie to his parents' home for a visit. The night before he was to head back to school, the sky darkened ominously and the weather turned ugly.

A ferocious blizzard blew in. Gordon's fears about driving through such potentially dangerous road conditions, combined with the constant racket of ice crystals pelting against his bedroom window, meant he barely slept a wink the night before he was to leave to return to school.

The next morning, despite his parents' expressions of concern, Gordon's own worries about the road conditions and his lack of sleep, Barrow set out.

In an attempt to quell his own worries as much as those of his parents, he assured his mother and father, "This parka's well-lined and it has a hood. My mitts and socks are the thick ones you knit for me last Christmas, Mom, and I have my work boots on. I'll be warm enough."

Gordon's father, perhaps wanting to put a positive voice to his desperate hopes for his son's safety added, "And the Jeep's as roadworthy a vehicle as you could drive."

The Barrows and their son exchanged desperately tight hugs before Gordon walked out of his parents' home. The noise of the storm overpowered their final good-byes to one another. The loving words were blown away by the swirling gales.

A moment later the young man turned the key in the Jeep's ignition and the engine sprang to life. He looked at his watch before backing away from the house and on to the road. It was nearly 8:00 in the morning but it was still dark as night. With this storm showing no signs of abating there would be very little light that day.

Even with the wipers rhythmically scraping across the vehicle's windshield and the headlights turned on, Gordon could see virtually nothing. He drove on, ever so slowly. He told himself that if he just managed to keep driving he would eventually get back to school safely.

I may never reach 25 miles per hour, he thought. *It'll take hours, but at least I'll get there.*

For hours, squinting into the pelting snow, Gordon drove at a virtual crawl along the highway, never once seeing another vehicle. To fight the loneliness that was beginning to crowd up against his feelings of fear, he began to talk out loud to himself. "Keep going, fella. You can do this." He repeated those words, hoping to prop up his unusually pessimistic outlook. "You've been through worse in the war and this time there's a great reward waiting for you at the end—a safe, warm dorm room and then, the next day interesting lectures in a room full of friendly classmates."

During the next hour he said those words, or similar ones, over and over again. They provided enough comfort to help suppress some of the increasing panic clambering up his throat—for a while.

Then, slowly at first, his self-administered assurances began to lose their effectiveness. The words were sounding hollow. As the hollowness increased they became a mocking echo. And Gordon Barrow realized that he was getting extremely sleepy. Continuing to drive was becoming even more dangerous. But how could he pull over to the curb and sleep? The snow was drifted and piled so high on the road that he had no idea where the highway's shoulder might be. Even if he could find the side of the road there would still be serious problems. If he turned the engine off he stood a very good chance of freezing to death. If he left the motor running he might run out of gas—at which point he'd certainly freeze to death anyway.

By now there were tears in Gordon's eyes—tears of terror—that obscured his vision completely. He eased up on
the accelerator, slowing the Jeep to less than 15 miles (24
kilometers) per hour.

And it was a good thing he did slow down, for not 10
feet (3 meters) ahead of him stood a man—a soldier!
Though Gordon didn't know where the soldier had come
from or how he had suddenly appeared, he was just happy
that he was there. Gordon slowed his car to a halt just a
few feet from the solitary man. His plan to stop and offer
help to the stranger was more self-serving than it might
have been if he hadn't been feeling so lonely and desperate. He reached over from the driver's seat and held open
the passenger door for the man who climbed out of the
storm and into the shelter of the vehicle.

"Hi!" Gordon greeted the man enthusiastically.

For a moment there was silence in the cab of the Jeep.

"You look very tired," the stranger said. "Would you
like me to drive for a while?"

"Yes. Yes, I would like a break from the driving. If I
look tired it's because I really am exhausted. I'm headed to
Laramie if that suits you."

The stranger nodded, got out of the Jeep and walked
around to the driver's seat. Gordon gratefully slid out
from underneath the steering wheel and over to the passenger's seat. The relief of not having to drive was all
encompassing. Gordon realized that he was completely
worn out. His head began to nod and within seconds his
chin was resting on his chest. In the final seconds before
he lost consciousness, he had an odd thought—the man
he'd picked up at the side of the deserted road looked

exactly like himself. The man's face was identical. Even the army uniform the man wore was familiar.

I must remember to mention the coincidence to him when I wake up, Gordon thought as the last threads of consciousness slipped from him completely.

The gentle rocking motion of the Jeep moving through the horrendous wind comforted Gordon. Its gentle rocking had a quality of déjà vu to it, but the man's ability to think that through was well beyond his reach right then.

Gordon Barrow slept deeply for over an hour, oblivious to the fact that he was in his vehicle and beside a truly extraordinary presence. It wasn't until the lulling sensation of movement stopped that Gordon finally awoke. The stranger, who was now sitting motionless in the driver's seat, had driven him to a crossroads just outside Laramie—roughly 40 miles (64 kilometers) from the University of Wyoming's campus. The life-threatening blizzard had either stopped or they'd driven out of it. What a relief!

As Gordon came fully awake he remembered his manners and rather than immediately asking if this kind stranger noticed any resemblance between the two of them, extended his sincere thanks for the help with the driving. He offered to take the man to wherever it was he needed to go.

"It's still cold and there are no towns for miles. Walking could be dangerous," Gordon pointed out.

"That's all right, my friend," the man replied. "I can make my way safely from here, as can you."

"Thank you again," Gordon Barrow called out as the man stepped out onto the road.

"You're welcome," the stranger replied before turning to wave at Gordon who, by then, was standing on the snow-packed road beside his Jeep, not 10 feet (3 meters) from the mysterious soldier. The stranger, Gordon Barrow realized with certainty, was really no stranger at all. It was Gordon Barrow himself. He was staring at a mirror image of himself. This could be no trick of light or optical illusion, for the entity was even clad in the uniform that Gordon had worn to do his duty during the Second World War. Gordon Barrow had somehow been rescued by a manifestation of himself.

For the rest of his life, recollections of that amazing experience were never far from Gordon Barrow's mind. He didn't bother telling many people about the enigmatic encounter and, to this day, no one, not even Gordon Barrow, knows for certain exactly what took place on Wyoming's roads that perilous day.

Had the young man at the side of the road really been an angel disguised in as familiar a form as possible to help guarantee Gordon Barrow's acceptance of the much-needed supernatural help? Or had the entity really been Gordon's spirit from those long war years? Had there somehow been a bend in time? Or perhaps Gordon was a surviving twin? Maybe he had a brother, unknown to him, who died and then had always been with him as a sort of ghostly guardian?

Or, of course, the skeptics might reason that Gordon Barrow simply lost consciousness during that horrible drive and dreamed the entire incident. That might be a possible explanation except that, when he woke up, the inexplicable image was still in the driver's seat, Gordon was still in the passenger's seat and they had somehow traveled quite a distance.

Gordon Barrow's extraordinary experience on the highway to Laramie that stormy night remains a complete mystery and one of the most often-told ghost stories of the Rocky Mountains.

Lingering Spirit

Living on, or even making your way along, the Oregon Trail in the 1840s was not for the faint of heart. Food and water sources along the route were drying up while the number of pioneers competing for those sources was increasing, leading to a dangerous situation. If Fort Boise, Idaho, and the soldiers who manned the post had not existed, the situation would have been even more hazardous. Miners, traders, settlers and thieves came from all over to exploit their various talents and the area.

By the mid-1840s, a man named Manuel Sato had made his way to the trail from Mexico. Details of this man's particular skills and ambitions have been lost in the mists of history. All that remains for us to know about are the last moments of Sato's life. And the first few years of his afterlife.

In the last hour of Sato's life, he prepared breakfast for himself. Unbeknownst to him, close by, a bank robber was skulking away from the site of his latest heist and toward Sato's temporary residence. Neither man knew of the other's existence. Sato planned to eat his morning meal and then immediately head back out on his journey along the trail. The robber intended to bury his stash of loot and simply lie low for a while.

As the thief created a hiding spot for the stolen cash, the noise he made attracted Sato's attention. Moments later the two caught sight of one another. Even in that split second, they both knew this was the end for one of them. The bank robber was quicker than the Mexican, and seconds later, Sato lay bleeding to death from one well-placed knife wound.

Soldiers from Fort Boise who were sent out to help chase down the bank robber discovered Sato's body and the buried loot. They were calm about their discovery. Examining crime scenes was exactly the kind of thing their guard station had been created to do, and the men were not the least bit frightened. Not, that is, until they were tying Sato's corpse onto a pack animal to take it back to the base. That is when one of the men let out a bloodcurdling scream. Sato's body may have been lashed onto the mule but his ghost was standing in front of them! The apparition of the dead man looked impossibly alive and looked as though he was trying to urge on a pack of mules.

Of course, there was no mule train. Not that they could see anyway. Nor, by that time, was there really any Manuel Sato. Not of this world anyway.

Despite Sato's untimely and criminal death that morning, the soldiers of Fort Boise continued to see his ghost until the fort was abandoned fully a decade later. Perhaps even today the Mexican's image might be visible—if you knew exactly where to look.

The Unscrupulous Colonel

In the mid-1800s, the search for gold brought many entrepreneurs to the Rocky Mountains. The trek itself killed many good people. Many others died of broken hearts, never able to establish or even find a potential source of wealth. Some were unscrupulous enough to avoid those pitfalls. These were "claim jumpers," crooks who simply waited until their law-abiding peers had found, and begun to work, a rich gold vein before over-powering the mine's rightful owners and claiming the cache for themselves. These thieves usually worked in groups of two or three.

Just after the Civil War, a trio of claim jumpers made their way to south-central Colorado, to the town of Rosita. Colonel Graham, Colonel Boyd and a man named W.A. Stewart wasted no time executing a hostile takeover of a reasonably successful mining operation. Perhaps the folks in Rosita were more easily offended than they were in other parts, or perhaps Graham, Boyd and Stewart's crime marked their breaking point. Whatever the case, the other men living and mining in and around Rosita were infuri-ated by these interloping thieves. They decided to retaliate by arming themselves and charging at the criminals.

The three outlaws fled in any direction they could, not one of them bothering to make sure either of the others was safe. Graham, who was described in a newspaper arti-cle from the era as being "as mild a man as ever scuttled a ship or slit a throat," sought refuge in a nearby building. Once he was safely hidden, he quickly verified that he hadn't lost his guns during his escape.

We don't know whether Colonel Graham was feeling desperate to come out of hiding or whether he merely had a stupidly overinflated sense of self-confidence, but we do know that after a very short time he emerged from his hiding place. Guns blazing, he charged out onto the street. Seconds later his body, riddled with dozens of bullets, lay bleeding in the dirt.

None of this is too surprising because so many tales of claim jumpers ended in a way similar to the scene described above. What makes this tale different is that this story did not end with Graham's death. For dozens of years people reported seeing the translucent figure of Colonel Graham wandering near the spot where he was gunned down that fateful day.

Eventually Rosita, Colorado, became a ghost town, and Graham may well have been the only "surviving" resident of the place. Today, the once-booming mining town is again flourishing. To date there have not been any sightings of the outlaw's image reported but, of course, that doesn't mean the town isn't still haunted.

Newly Haunted

Most haunted venues in the Rocky Mountains have long and colorful histories. Such legacies make it easy to understand why there are so many ghost stories connected to those places. For this reason, perhaps you wouldn't expect there to be a ghost story in Kananaskis Country, an hour's drive west of Calgary. The area, approximately 1500 square miles (4000 square kilometers), includes the alpine ski facility developed for the 1988 Winter Olympic Games. Fortunately for those who prefer their winter wonderlands to be peaceful, this resort region is still not as crowded as Banff and Jasper, the two more established Rocky Mountain parks nearby.

A hotel in Kananaskis Country that provides every amenity a guest could ask for employs a large staff. Among the many workers at that hotel a few years ago was a chef's assistant. The man was known as a loner but he worked, seemingly happily enough, at his job for a number of years. This routine continued right up to one autumn afternoon when he failed to report for work.

Colleagues checked his quarters in the staff residence building but could not find the man. His room looked as though he'd just left it and fully intended to be back shortly. There was no sign that he had moved out, nor were there any clues as to where he might be. For a while, no one did anything. After all, the man was an adult well able to make his own choices about his life. If he had decided to go somewhere else rather than show up for his shift at work, there wasn't very much any one could do about it—at least not right then. When some time had gone by, however, the people who knew the man became concerned and phoned the Royal Canadian Mounted Police. The Mounties took the report and searched the area but could not find any trace of the man.

As days turned into weeks, a few of the hotel employees began to think that they'd seen the missing man. Each time they thought they had spotted him, he'd been walking along the highway either to or from the hotel and, oddly, was wearing his kitchen uniform. Initially no one mentioned seeing this strange sight to anyone else at the hotel. Privately they were worried that their description of what they'd seen would sound foolish. Finally, though, the workers who'd thought they'd seen him began to share their suspicions with one another.

"Maybe he needs help," one staff member suggested.

The others agreed that was a possibility. At first they merely kept a closer look out for the man as they drove the route. When that wasn't effective they organized a search party and set out to look for him.

They hadn't driven very far when first one person and then all of them caught a glimpse of the man they were looking for. As with every time they'd seen him, he was striding along the shoulder of the highway. The group pulled their cars over and ran toward the man, calling his name. As they came within a few feet of this familiar human figure, one that they were all sure they had seen, it vaporized before their eyes.

Badly shaken, the people in the group drove away to find a spot where they could sit and discuss what they'd just witnessed. All agreed on the details. It was definitely their former coworker whom they had seen each time—

this time included. They also agreed that he had simply, and impossibly, vanished into thin air.

Despite some fear of ridicule, they knew they would have to notify the police again. After being directed to the spot on the highway where the hotel staff had seen the image walking, the police headed away from the road and into the dense forest.

The police did find the missing man—or at least his corpse. Investigation revealed that he had set up a makeshift campsite just in from the area of the highway where his illusion had been seen. When the site and the man's remains were examined, it was determined that there had been no foul play associated with the death. There was also no evidence at all that he'd been wearing his uniform from work when he left the hotel premises. It was interesting then that his ghost was.

Shortly after the grisly discovery, the man's family was informed and his body was respectfully buried. Since then there have been no further reports of the ghostly kitchen worker walking beside the highway in Kananaskis Country. Of course, that's not to say that the apparition is not still walking, nor that people have not seen him. It's possible that many folks have seen the ghost but none have reported it publicly.

Sorrowful Spirits

Two rather similar ghost legends exist—both in Idaho but miles apart.

The first tale involves a waterfall on the Snake River just at the point where the river forges its way through Fremont County. It is said that if whitewater adventurers are in danger, the image of a beautiful woman dressed in white emerges from the mist. If there is time, she will warn the travelers not to proceed any farther. If there isn't time she will somehow reposition the craft they're in so that they can make it to safety.

This lifesaving ghost has been haunting that spot on the river for hundreds of years. Legend says that when she was alive the woman watched in horror as the man she loved was swept to his death by the current. Her mission in the afterlife seems to be to prevent the heavy currents from claiming any more lives.

Much farther north, in the Idaho panhandle near the Montana border, there is an even sadder ghost story. Apparently for hundreds of years the ghost of a beautiful, broken-hearted maiden has been seen on Spirit Lake. The apparition is crystal clear to all those who see her. She usually appears on moonlit nights, has long flowing black hair and sits completely immobile in a phantom canoe.

This ghostly scene has been reported every now and again since the moonlit night when a warrior was killed in battle. His bride-to-be was so completely devastated by her mourning that one night she paddled out to the middle of the lake. By the light of the full moon she threw

If they run into trouble, whitewater adventurers in Idaho can rely on the help of a woman in white who emerges from the mist.

herself into the waters and ended her life—in this realm. The intensity of the girl's sorrow must have imprinted itself on the very atmosphere at that spot so that her grief still reverberates on the waters.

The Three Nephites

When dealing with the paranormal, things are often not as well defined as we'd like them to be. What, for instance, constitutes a "true" ghost story? Is a person's paranormal experience less valid if there is no official documentation to verify the encounter? And when is a ghost story not a ghost story at all? Are the many tales of vanishing hitchhikers ghost stories or are they urban legends?

Whichever category you may wish to place them in, these morality tales come from various parts of the world and often include many of the following details. A person who is driving a car sees an image at the side of the road. The driver stops to give the apparently stranded stranger a lift. Sometimes, just at that moment, the hitchhiker simply vanishes. Other times it is reported that the apparition enters the car but then vanishes shortly after. Often these intriguing stories have added twists—the hitchhiker might have left a belonging, often a sweater, in the Good Samaritan's car. When the concerned driver tries to return that belonging he's told that the person who owns the sweater, the individual he gave the lift to, died many years before. That, certainly, is a ghost story, but how do you account for the fact that the driver is still holding a very real sweater in his hand?

These next stories are like those. They don't exactly fit the category of either ghost story or urban legend—although some of them do include the vanishing hitchhiker component. And each of them is just too good a story not to include. For convenience, perhaps we should refer to these sorts of supernatural stories as ghostly legends.

According to the *Book of Mormon*, Christ visited South America immediately after his crucifixion in the Holy Land. When He was there, just as He had in the eastern part of the world, Jesus apparently chose apostles to help Him on this second ministry. Upon their deaths, most of His western-world apostles requested that they go to heaven. Three of the followers asked that they be allowed to stay on earth into eternity. Their wish, according to Chapter 28, Nephi in the *Book of Mormon*, was granted, and even today these miraculous men, known as the Three Nephites (pronounced "Knee-Fights") are said to walk among us.

Whether these miraculous Nephites are here on earth merely as apparitions or whether they are actually physical bodies has been widely debated. So, of course, has their origin and even their very existence. As a result, this is a controversial, but fascinating, area of inquiry.

Probably because the Church of Jesus Christ of Latter-Day Saints (the Mormon Church) was settled in Salt Lake City, the following stories about the Three Nephites take place around that area.

The first anecdote contains many legendary elements and probably took place on a southbound stretch of Highway 15 in Utah. Unfortunately, the date of this sighting was not recorded but the details that remain do lead one to suspect that the hitchhiker might have been one of the Three Nephites.

As a couple drove away from a location just south of Salt Lake City, they were most surprised to see an old man standing at the side of the deserted highway. When they drew nearer to the image they could see that he was trying to thumb a lift. Though not in the habit of giving rides to strangers, they were afraid that if they didn't pick up this man, someone less scrupulous might.

The driver slowed the car, pulled off to the side of the road and then began to back up so that the elderly man would not have too far to walk to their car. As he climbed into the back seat, the man expressed his gratitude for their kindness in stopping for them. As they pulled back onto the highway and continued to drive south, they enjoyed a lively discussion with their new rider. Eventually, though, the conversation slowed and in time they were enjoying a companionable silence in the car.

Some moments later the driver decided it was time to chat again. When his initial comment did not garner a reply he stole a glance back to where the old fellow had been sitting. Seconds later he swerved to the shoulder of the road and hit the brake pedal—hard. The back seat was completely empty.

"This can't be!" he exclaimed, staring with utter disbelief into the empty area.

"Where could he have gone?" the driver's wife wondered. "We haven't stopped the car!"

Realizing that their comments to one another were never going to solve this mystery, they simply sat in silence for a while and tried to accept that a paranormal event had occurred in their presence.

After a few minutes, the man drove the car back onto the highway and headed for the next town where they stopped for a bite to eat.

"Let's ask the waitress if she's ever heard of anyone like that man," the driver's wife suggested. Her husband nodded his head silently.

Smiling ever so slightly, the waitress listened to the woman's description of the strange man they'd picked up and how he had, impossibly, vanished from their car as they drove along a highway at approximately 70 miles (100 kilometers) per hour.

"I've never seen him myself," the server replied, "but I do know that a woman in town saw a man who looked just like the one you're describing. She said that he asked her for some food. She gave it to him of course. He took it and turned to walk away. As he receded into the distance she swears he simply vaporized."

The offer or request of food is a common factor in the stories about the Three Nephites. Many of the encounters involving these supernatural beings involve people giving their strange intruder a meal. This next story is an excellent example of such an incident.

Again the location of these events was Utah. The time is reported in one rendition of the ghostly legend to have been "a hot summer day in the year 1874."

Edwin and Lyda Squires and their three young daughters lived in a tiny shack some distance east of Salt Lake City. They made their living by keeping horses and cattle. On the day that the strange event took place, Edwin had gone to round up some cattle. Mrs. Squires stayed behind in the house to look after the little girls.

"I'll be back by 7:00," the man informed his wife as he kissed her good-bye before leaving the house.

The girls and their mother spent a pleasant day together, and by about 6:00 the children helped their mother begin to prepare the evening meal. When Edwin Squires was not back home by 8:00 they became concerned and went out of the house to look for the man. They couldn't see him but, oddly, there was another man walking toward their humble home.

"Could you give me a meal?" the stranger asked Mrs. Squires. She didn't know what to do. Would it be dangerous to take this man in or would it be cruel to send a hungry man on his way when she had food ready on the table? After a few seconds she decided that she couldn't let the man continue on without food. After all, there wasn't another house for miles.

The frightened woman invited the man to come in and sit down at their table. He had gray hair, a long white beard and was dressed neatly. It was his eyes, though, that really attracted Mrs. Squires' attention. Later she told a friend, "his eyes were so bright that they twinkled when he talked." At first he didn't say a word but simply ate the food that had been set down in front of him. Eventually, though, he began to talk. In an account written in 1943, an acquaintance of the Squires, a woman named Mrs. Elzina Robison (or possibly Robinson), of Bunkerville, Nevada, indicated that the conversation went like this:

"He conversed with Mrs. Squires and said, 'Sister, you are not well.' She said 'No, I am not. I have a pain under my shoulder, which bothers me a great deal.' He said 'That is your liver, but don't worry. You won't be bothered by that anymore.' "

Mrs. Robison continued with the account, "Then the strange man got up and started off. He thanked her for her kindness and for the fine meal. As he was leaving he said, 'God bless you, Sister. You will never want for anything. You will always be blessed with plenty.' Then he left. Mrs. Squires rushed to the window in order to see what direction the strange man was heading but he was gone. There was simply no sign of him."

Understandably upset by the bizarre visitor and even more so by his disappearance, the woman stood still for a moment. Then, not knowing what else to do, she turned back to the table in preparation to clear away the empty plates the old man had eaten from. According to Mrs. Robison's report, Mrs. Squires found "the table was still just as she had set it" even though she had sat there and watched as the man had eaten the food she'd put on the plates and drunk the milk she'd put in his glass."

A few minutes later Edwin Squires returned home safe and sound. He was so pleased with the way his day had gone that Mrs. Squires didn't want to burden him by describing the strange experience she'd just had. Then, when a few days passed and she still hadn't said anything, she decided it was best just to keep the story to herself.

For months Mrs. Squires didn't tell a soul about the eerie events from that evening, but she was not able to put the incident out of her mind. Eventually, the woman decided to confide in her mother, Mrs. Abigail Abbott. The older woman was swift in announcing her assessment of the encounter. "Why Lyda, that was one of the Three Nephites who dined at your table."

And Mrs. Abbott may well have been correct because from that time on the Squires never wanted for a thing. Mrs. Squires lived to nearly 90 and left enough material resources for her children and grandchildren to have a more than good life. This fact was confirmed by a man named Bowman who married one of Lyda and Edwin Squires' daughters.

The next anecdote does not involve food but, once again, a couple driving on a deserted section of road offering a strange-looking hitchhiker a ride. The incident took place early in 1944.

A couple driving in a truck came upon a man standing at the side of the road. He appeared to be very old, and, as there were no towns nearby, the couple decided to stop and offer him a lift. As the three drove along they chatted about many events. The stranger seemed to be especially well versed on the current volatile political situation.

Sometime later, the man asked to be let out of the truck at a particularly desolate point in the landscape.

"But there's nothing here, sir," the driver noted with concern. "Why don't we at least take you to the next town?"

The hitchhiker assured the couple that he would be fine there, so the driver slowed the vehicle, pulled over to the side of the road and let the man out. After thanking the people for their kind assistance the man offered the following predictions: "The war will end in August. On your return trip you will be hauling a corpse."

The weird encounter gave the couple lots to talk about until they reached their destination. Once there, they attended to the business that had taken them away from home in the first place and then headed back. About halfway home they stopped at the scene of a tragic accident and offered to assist in anyway they could.

"There's a small village not far up the road. Take this body there and let someone know about the accident."

The couple nodded silently as those who had arrived on the scene ahead of them lifted the body into the bed of their pickup truck.

As they drove away from the accident, the man asked his wife, "How could that hitchhiker possibly have known this was going to happen?" But the woman was too upset to speak and merely shook her head.

By the time autumn came the couple who'd had the eerie experience with the stranger and the corpse had put the incident out of their minds as much as they possibly could. Then, one day the man said to his wife, "August has come and gone and there's not been an end to the war. It must just have been a fluke that the man we picked up at the side of the road a few months back knew we'd be asked to transport a body that day."

This time his wife's only response was a silent nod of agreement. They said nothing more about that day in 1944—until August of 1945, when the war ended. With that coincidence they determined that the man they'd driven in their truck had been one of the Three Nephites.

As we might surmise from the tales related above, the Nephites usually appear singly, but a few reports have them together.

In Holden, Utah, three elderly men appeared in the home of a woman whose baby was deathly ill. The trio went straight to the ailing infant's crib and began to tend to the child. They seemed to fuss over the baby for a while before circling the child's bed and praying. Moments later they disappeared as mysteriously and suddenly as they appeared. Before daybreak the infant was completely well and from that day until old age, the child who had been attended to by the three apparitions was never sick again.

A similar incident occurred right in Salt Lake City. Mr. and Mrs. Price, their son John, John's wife, Isabella, and their infant son all lived together. The baby had been seriously ill for sometime. Neither medical treatments nor prayer sessions seemed to make any difference. The child's condition did nothing but worsen.

The family was extremely distressed, so when a knock came at their door late one evening they were initially not very pleased about it. When they opened the door and discovered an elderly man in a gray suit asking for entry they were even less comfortable. The man told the people that he needed shelter for the night. The Prices said that they had no extra beds, but as it was so late, they didn't want to turn the man away completely.

"If you wish to doze by our fire then you are welcome," John Price informed the stranger, who gratefully accepted. John and Isabella took their ailing child and retired for the evening.

Grandpa Price was leery of leaving someone they didn't know alone in their home, so he curled up in a chair in the corner of the living room, intending to stay awake all night. However, exhaustion won out and he did eventually fall asleep.

Several hours later Grandma Price pulled herself out of a dead sleep. Something in the house didn't sound right. There were noises coming from the main room of her son's home—sounds she didn't recognize. She padded her way to the doorway leading to that room. The stranger was sitting at the younger Price's table but the table looked different. Instead of being bare, the rough wood was covered by a beautiful white tablecloth—a tablecloth so white it fairly glowed. The man was eating a piece of bread but this was not the humble wheat bread that the Prices had on hand. It was a piece of white bread—bread as white as the tablecloth—bread so white its glow was actually painful for the older woman to look at.

Grandma was startled by the sight, but she didn't think that anyone in the household was in any sort of danger, so she made her way back to bed.

The next morning Isabella Price invited the old man in the gray suit to join them for breakfast. He declined, saying that he was sure the food would be wonderful but that he had no time to stay. He thanked them for their hospitality and left as mysteriously as he had arrived. Seconds later they heard their child cooing and giggling in its crib. As John and his parents stayed to watch the man walk away, Isabella went to the baby's room. Seconds later all four adults were talking at once. The baby's mother was astonished and delighted to discover that the baby had suddenly made a miraculous recovery. John and his parents were eager to tell the young woman that the strange visitor had walked about 10 feet (3 meters) before disappearing before their eyes. The Prices and everyone in their neighborhood have been convinced from that moment on that they had been visited by a Nephite.

Near Holden, just to the west of Utah's Wasatch Plateau, a man named John Rogers is sure that he talked with one of the Three Nephites. He had seen an old man standing at the side of the road and presumed that the man needed some assistance. He stopped his vehicle, got out and walked the few feet back to the old man, who politely informed Rogers that he was fine and didn't require any help. The two chatted for a time at the side of the road. Once Rogers was content that the old man would be all right, he bid him good-bye and turned to get back into this car. A few seconds later, Rogers had gone only a few feet when it crossed his mind to ask just one last time if the man could use a drive. The man he had been talking to just moments before had vanished. In this case we have no follow-up report except that the elderly man in question has always been presumed to have been one of the Nephites.

One of the Three Nephites has been known to suddenly appear where an accident has occurred too. Once, a 12-year-old boy who was helping his father with some chores cut his arm very badly. Before his father even had time to run to his son's side, an old man appeared. The mysterious being placed his thumb directly on the deep cut and kept it there as the father and son stared in amazement. Once the blood flow was controlled, he bandaged the wound. Before disappearing he instructed the boy, "Don't touch that hand for three weeks."

The child nodded his agreement as his father watched in mute amazement. Three weeks later, they took the bandages off. The wound had healed without leaving so much as a scar.

And now, two final stories about the Nephites. Niels Nielsen was out in his barn late one evening. He had some work to attend to there but was eager to get back to the house where his wife had warm milk waiting for him. Suddenly someone appeared at the barn door. At first Nielsen presumed it was his wife but when she didn't say anything to him he looked around. The person standing in the doorway was most assuredly not his wife. It was a tall man beside a rickety old cart that was hooked up to two decrepit-looking horses.

"What can I do for you?" Nielsen asked in a slightly angry tone of voice.

"I've come nearly 100 miles [160 kilometers]," the man said before adding, "I need a place to rest for the night."

Nielsen was very skeptical of the man's word. No one could have traveled even 10 miles (16 kilometers) with that dilapidated old buggy and those scrawny horses. Still, he felt he couldn't turn the man away. It was fully dark and would be dangerous for the man to go any farther.

"All right," Nielsen agreed. "Come, let's stable your horses and then I'll take you in to meet my wife. If you're hungry, she was just fixing me a bedtime snack and I'm sure there'll be enough to share."

Moments later the two men walked into the house. Her husband's guest made Mrs. Nielsen very nervous but she served him a meal and a beverage anyway. *Lord knows*, she thought, *he looks as though he needs the nourishment.* As the men sat down at the table, the newcomer's conversation did nothing to assuage Mrs. Nielsen's feeling of unease. He spoke of having been turned down for food and accommodation at other homes along the way.

"They'll be sorry," he stated threateningly before telling the couple about some of his recent travels. By this time Mrs. Nielsen was really uncomfortable about having this man in her home. She did not believe one word he said about having been in New York, London and even Vienna, so she decided to try to trick him.

"Have you ever been to Atchison, Kansas?" she asked in supposed innocence. Atchison had been her hometown until she'd married Niels and moved west.

"I have," he acknowledged before launching into descriptions of the current lives of people he knew there. Every person the man mentioned was someone Mrs. Nielsen had known well.

That night as she lay in bed unable to sleep, Mrs. Nielsen wondered over and over again about the coincidence of this man, who apparently knew all her old friends, arriving at her house looking for hospitality. The next morning she was tired from a lack of sleep but got out of bed in time to offer the man a hearty breakfast before he left. The man declined her offer but did agree to take a lunch that she had packed along on his journey in the rickety old cart with the feeble-looking horses.

Minutes after his image disappeared over the crest of a hill, neighbors of the Nielsens arrived at their door.

"You must have passed an old man driving a dreadful looking cart as you came here," she announced to her early morning visitors.

"No," they replied with complete assuredness. "We saw no one on the road."

Now Mrs. Nielsen was even more puzzled. There was only one road to take from their farm. They had seen the man steering his cart along there and the neighbors would definitely have been on the same stretch of lane at the same time. It would have been impossible for them not to have seen the odd old man as he made his way from their home—unless, of course, he had simply disappeared.

Neither the Nielsens nor their neighbors ever solved that mystery. As the years went along, though, it became apparent that the people who had been approached by the old man that night and had turned down his request for food and shelter did not prosper. The Nielsens, whose circumstances at the time of the stranger's visit had been all but identical to their neighbors,' had seemed blessed, and their well-being flourished. As the community was made up mostly of Mormons it soon became an accepted fact that the Nielsens had hosted a visit from one of the Three Nephites.

Mr. Rencher, a Mormon farmer in Utah, was driving his horse-drawn tractor down a country road when he came to a man walking at the side of the road.

"I can give you a lift," he called out to the walker. "It's not very comfortable and it's not very fast but it's better than walking."

The man smiled and climbed up on the metal spring-loaded seat beside the driver. The two began to chat and inevitably the chatter turned to the topic of religion. Rencher's passenger seemed to know more about the *Book of Mormon* than anyone the farmer had ever met before. The discussion continued until Rencher came within sight of his farm and his new friend asked to be let off.

"I can offer you a bed for the night," Rencher said.

"No, thank you sir," came the reply. "I'll be fine."

As he climbed down from the tractor, the horses pulling the contraption suddenly reared up. It took all of Rencher's efforts and concentration to calm the animals.

That's so strange, he thought. *These animals are always calm. I've never had them act up like this.*

By the time he had the steeds safely calmed, the old man who'd been with him had disappeared.

The next day when Rencher was in town he stopped to talk to some of the people whose homes he'd passed when he'd been giving the stranger a ride. They all remembered seeing him sitting on his tractor and being pulled by his horses, but no one had seen anyone sitting with Rencher. They all swore that they knew for a fact Rencher had been alone in the wagon when he'd ridden past their houses. Rencher was equally certain that at those moments he had been with a man so knowledgeable about religion that Rencher was sure he could never forget him.

Are those encounters true ghost stories, modern myths or ghostly legends? Perhaps it doesn't really matter at all what you call them as long as you realize the significance of the amazing events those people experienced close to the Rocky Mountains.

Tragic Llorona

Not all ghost stories fit neatly into one specific classification or another. The following old (and current!) tale is certainly difficult to categorize. Is it a religious story, a morality tale, a myth or simply one of the many true ghost stories from the Rocky Mountains? Perhaps you might be able to decide after reading about La Llorona—The Weeping Woman.

Hispanic folk history tells us that in the days when the conquistadors rode through the southwestern United States there was one exceptionally gorgeous young peasant woman. She was tall and had long, flowing, jet black hair. By the time the girl was in her mid-teens she had discovered the power of her appearance and had learned well how to exploit the scores of men who were drawn to her.

The girl's family pleaded with her to change her sinful ways before it was too late and she ruined her life. Sadly, she would not listen to them, so by day she lived the life of a struggling peasant on the banks of the Santa Fe River but in the evening she danced with wealthy men in the finest establishments.

Over the years she bore two sons—gorgeous little boys who had inherited their mother's exceptional appearance and lighthearted attitude. They were a joy to behold and everyone in the village by the river doted on the children. Everyone, that is, except their mother. The selfish woman ignored the boys completely, leaving them to be looked after by her mother.

One evening as the neglectful mother prepared to leave her family's home for another night of riotous living, the little boys chased after her. "Don't leave us!" they entreated, but to no avail. Some time later, both were discovered face down in the river. No one ever knew for certain what had happened to cause the little fellows to drown. Perhaps they had been running too fast and were therefore not able to stop. Perhaps they had been so hurt by their mother's rejection of them that they threw themselves into the river to their death. Or, perhaps, as some would have us believe, they were drowned by their mother.

We do know that the boys' deaths tortured the wayward woman and brought about her own premature demise. She was never again seen inside the fancy dance halls that had drawn her from her sons. Instead, the heartbroken mother spent the rest of her life roaming the riverbank where her sons had perished. It is said that from the day of their deaths she never ate or rested. Those who saw her during her final days attested that such was clearly the case. She became pathetically thin and malnourished, her clothes became ragged and she became mute from days and days of wailing in emotional agony.

Within a matter of months the once-flamboyant woman lay dead on the bank of the river that had stolen her sons' last breaths. Her remains were interred in a burial ground near the river where her sons had died.

Tragically, even death has not healed the woman's tortured soul. For her image is still seen by people of Hispanic descent. The tragic form forlornly floats about the Santa Fe area of New Mexico and has also been seen, among other places, in Pueblo, Colorado. The ghost is easily recognizable by her sorrowful demeanor and once-gorgeous long, black locks. In death her voice has been restored and witnesses say her wails pierce their hearts. Worse, encountering La Llorona, or The Weeping Woman as she has been appropriately dubbed, seems to foretell disaster to those who see her.

In the 1930s an old man was standing outside his home in Santa Fe chatting with a neighbor when he saw a movement in his peripheral vision. Patricio Lujan spun around to see what it was. The man was most disturbed to realize that La Llorona was coming toward him. The entity floated across the river toward him before disappearing for a few seconds. Soon the spirit reappeared and continued toward Lujan and his friend. Hoping that they were mistaken, that their visitor was just an ordinary flesh-and-blood woman, they stood silently and watched her form approach them.

When they heard her wails, however, they could not deny that they had seen the ghost so many others had talked about. Her feet didn't quite reach the ground, and she hovered just above the earth. Patricio Lujan prepared for the inevitable. He knew that within days tragedy would strike his life, and it did. A young and previously healthy family member died just a few days later without apparent cause.

A few years later, Judith Beatty and her husband, Edward Garcia Kraul, bought Lujan's house. Edward's association with the legendary ghost went back to childhood when his great uncle had reportedly seen the specter. The ghost had apparently warned the man to stop being rude to his mother. She threatened that she would continue to haunt him if he continued his disrespectful ways. The man heeded the supernatural warning, mended his ways and lived the rest of his long life in peace and harmony.

Having grown up knowing this story, Edward had believed in and greatly respected the ghost and her powers. In order to honor her existence and possibly to protect himself and his wife from the ghost's powers, he named his home "La Casa de la Llorona."

In 1954, the enduring phantom was seen once again, this time in Pueblo, Colorado. JoAnn was a teenager at the time and had just traveled with family from New Mexico north to Avondale, very near Pueblo. They settled in one of the many riverside houses built to accommodate migrant workers. One night, just after midnight, the entire community was wakened by horrid screams and moans. The dreadful sounds seemed to be coming from the nearby river. JoAnn, her family members and neighbors rushed to the water to see if they could help the person in distress. Once they got there, they had the impression that the screams were emanating from the opposite bank. Several men made their way across the river but found there was no one on that shore either. Even more puzzling was that once they were on that side of the river, the shrieks seemed to be coming from the other.

JoAnn recalled that the men crossed the river back and forth several times before giving up and accepting that the cries they were hearing were not from either side of the river but from the other side of the curtain of time. These were the phantom moans of the long-deceased La Llorona.

Tragedy may have struck more of the witnesses that night, but as JoAnn was the source of this information and her family was untouched, we cannot know for certain.

Today, in Santa Fe, New Mexico, a building stands where La Llorona was buried so many years ago. Many people of Hispanic descent will not go into that building because they have heard tales that the place is haunted—haunted by the sad spirit of the shameless mother. Perhaps these folks are being overly cautious, but it is hard to fault them when you learn that security guards have heard mournful sobbing coming from everywhere and nowhere in the building. Or that workers have felt themselves being pushed by an invisible hand when they were standing at the top of a staircase. Especially convincing is the experience that a woman named Henrietta Stockell had in 1981 on the third floor of the building.

Stockell was apparently working with her back to the door of a particular room when she heard the elevator arrive on the third floor. The woman called out a greeting, thinking that it was one of her colleagues looking for her for some reason or another. When Henrietta didn't get a response to her salutation, she walked out into the hallway. There she saw the impossible—a slightly transparent image of a woman gliding down the corridor. The startled worker later described the image as a tall and extraordinarily beautiful woman, with long black hair. Henrietta ran toward the being, but it vanished before her eyes. To this day the woman is sure she saw the presence of La Llorona walking the third-floor hallway in a building near the Santa Fe River.

This enduring ghost story is indeed intriguing. The Weeping Woman's image has been seen as far away as the banks of the Yellowstone River in Billings, Montana. Those who have encountered La Llorona do not worry that their experience does not fit into any particular category. They just know that they have been visited by a soul whose suffering is eternal.

Well-Timed Haunting

If you want the best chance to witness "living history," make a point to be in Wyoming on Highway 26 between Fort Laramie and Torrington sometime during 2004. That is when the ghost of a young woman is next expected to appear.

That portion of Highway 26 was once part of the Oregon Trail. During the mid-1800s, thousands and thousands of explorers, pioneers and settlers took the trail to cross the Rocky Mountains on their way to the coast. The route was the best available at the time but was difficult and dangerous. Many lived to settle in the homesteads they had sought, but many others who ventured out died tragic and premature deaths.

There is a fascinating haunting near the old trail between Fort Laramie and Torrington. Interestingly this ghostly vision is seen regularly—but only once every seven years. Though the ghost's appearances have been intermittent, she has been seen by numerous people, and the pattern to her haunting is remarkably unchanged.

Her elegant clothes indicate that this is not the ghost of a rough-living explorer. This ghost wears a feathered hat and green velvet riding clothes while sitting astride a jet black horse. She drives the animal on by whipping its flanks with a jeweled strap.

Many skilled horsemen on speedy mounts have tried to catch the girl, but they have never succeeded, no matter how hard or for what distance they drive their steeds. She never seems to change her speed but always manages to stay exactly the same distance away from her pursuers.

The legend says that the girl and her horse died hundreds of years ago. Her father told her she should not ride by herself, but she defiantly disobeyed her father's orders and rode out to explore the glorious countryside. As history teaches us, that was the girl's last ever ride—in life. Her disobedience was fatal, but the spirit of the girl and her loyal horse continue to charge into the future and are still seen—but just every seven years.

Whenever you can make it—2004, 2011, 2018—no doubt the long-deceased girl will still be making her regularly scheduled ride into eternity.

On The Road—Again

Working in a haunted building could certainly have its challenges, but at least employees would never be bored! If the ghosts started following the staff home, though, the employees might not be so agreeable. That, it seems, was the case at the Hotel Colorado where, over the hotel's long history, its spirits have occasionally gone along for a ride.

Richard, a security guard at the hotel, had experienced enough ghostly encounters at work that he was easily able to tell a haunted building from an unhaunted one. For this reason, he knew that his house was his and his alone and that there were no ghosts there. Except for the evening that a workplace revenant decided it needed a change of scenery and followed the man home.

He didn't indicate whether he was aware of the ghostly presence as he made the drive, but as soon as Richard walked into his home, he immediately noticed extraordinary differences. His stereo, for instance, continually turned on and off even though no one was near it. As Richard changed out of his uniform and into more comfortable clothing, he accidentally broke the nametag that the hotel supplied. He was annoyed with himself for what he considered carelessness and intended to try to repair the tag as soon as he finished changing, but just seconds later, he could not find either piece of the badge. No sooner had he given up hunting for the tag than it appeared on the floor at his feet—impossibly, in one piece.

Fortunately for Richard and all the other employees, most often when they order the entities back to the hotel where they "live," the ghosts obey. The encounter an employee named Dave had illustrates this point well. Dave knew that one of the manifestations from the haunted hotel had gone home with him when he saw his belongings, including large pieces of furniture, moving about the house—when no one was anywhere near them. Dave ordered the spirit to leave his house, and all returned to normal.

A hostess from the restaurant's night shift is sure that the spirit of a man walked her home one evening. Although that might be construed as a gentlemanly gesture, this woman did not take it that way because she had been bothered all evening by the feeling that something—something she could not see—had been watching her. That night the worker experienced a dreadful nightmare and always credited the ghost's unpleasant presence as the cause.

To read about the ghosts that stay on the Hotel Colorado's premises, see the story "Walter" in the chapter in this book entitled The Spirit's Inn.

Stallion Spirit

At daybreak on August 31, 1870, three cowboys—Ben, Frank and Stan—set out as the others in their camp were just waking up. The night before, the trio had been instructed to ride ahead of the other cattle drivers and the herd to scout for the safest and quickest route through the Owyhee area of Idaho.

They began their journey in good moods, but by noon that day felt only grim determination. By evening that grim determination turned to anger and frustration.

"We're lost," Ben stated flatly. "I have no idea where we are, where we should be or where the others are."

Frank added, to no one in particular, "If it wasn't cloudy we'd be better off. We could get our bearings from the sun."

Stan, in keeping with his way, stayed silent.

Frank continued, pointing toward the horizon as he spoke. "All we can do is keep heading that way. I think it's west and that's where the wintering grounds are. At least we have a couple more hours before night falls. A month from now it'd be so dark we'd be stranded here for the night."

The three men, all experienced cowboys, rode on through the bleak landscape. *Surely,* Stan thought, *the site we're searching for can't be too far from here.*

Despite the long, late-summer day, the three were even more disoriented and discouraged by the time the darkening sky forced them to stop for the night. They set up camp and fixed themselves some food before spreading out their bedrolls. Although they said nothing to one another, each wondered if this mission would prove to be the death of them. They had not seen even one settler or trapper since they left the other drivers and the cattle they were responsible for. Perhaps, each wondered, they never would see another human face again—ever. Perhaps this would be their last ride.

Hours later, the three men awoke to a still-cloudy dawn. After grabbing leftovers from dinner to eat in the first hour of that day's ride, they broke camp and continued to head west.

"These low-lying clouds are going to be the death of us," Ben predicted.

He had no way of knowing that he was just as wrong as could be in that statement. The presence of the clouds would, indirectly, play a huge role in their survival.

By late afternoon they stopped to give their mounts a rest and to fix themselves another meal. They were glum as they sat around the campfire, especially as they knew their day was long from over. They had more difficult riding ahead of them and not one of the three felt anything even approaching optimism about the immediate future.

Staying where they were, though, would bring certain death from starvation, so they forced themselves to prepare for another few hours' ride. All the while, not one said anything at all to the other.

Not, that is, until the stony silence was broken by Stan shrieking at the top of his lungs. "Thunderin' tarnation! Lord save me! Have I lost my mind? What's that? Over there? Coming from the bright spot between the clouds?"

When his partners took their eyes off their usually silent coworker, they turned their heads to look in the direction Stan was pointing. There, impossibly, was an enormous, pure white stallion. Its mane and tale were stretching out behind it as it flew—yes—flew, through a crack in the cloud cover. Frozen in shock, the three men stood beside their own horses and stared, their mouths hanging open.

Seconds later, an entire herd of horses also appeared from the clouds, following the huge stallion's airborne path. The trailing horses galloped clear of the clouds and charged on. They ran not on the earth but just over its surface. They were heading straight toward Ben, Stan and Fred. The men knew beyond a doubt that these horses could not be from this world. They grabbed hold of their own horses' reins, fearing the animals would be terrified and bolt, but their steeds did not show any reaction to the impossible scene bounding toward them.

"We need to follow!" Stan yelled.

The men jumped on their horses and rode at a dangerous, breakneck speed along the route the phantom herd was guiding them. Less than an hour later they pulled their horses to a stop. They were approaching a small settlement. They were saved. Their saviors, however, had disappeared between two clouds, almost into the proverbial "thin air."

Residents of the little camp who had heard the noise of the three men and their horses came out of their makeshift dwellings and greeted the men. The three confused cowboys tried to explain what had just happened to them, why they were there and why they had been riding so hard.

Those helping them wipe down their mounts were not surprised. The ghost of the white stallion and the herd of phantom horses were well known in the area. The animals had been saving lost souls by leading them to safety for years, apparently.

Some say even today, if you're lost in the Rocky Mountains' "Hawaii" (Owyhee County, Idaho), those same amazing ghostly images will appear to you too. Follow the phantoms. Their mission in death is to save the living.

3

The Spirit's Inn

*Hotels, motels, inns, boardinghouses—
they all serve as homes away from home
when we need them. Apparently, however,
not every guest checks out.*

Loving Illusion

Just south of Rocky Mountain National Park in Colorado lies the town of Black Hawk. The place is home to at least one ghost, a ghost with a romantic nature, a ghost who came courting. Although information about precisely what year, or years, these romantic encounters took place is no longer known, the other details of the stories remain.

One night, a woman we'll call Doreen lay sleeping in a rented room in a Black Hawk rooming house. She was awakened by a strange and decidedly uncomfortable sensation—the sensation that she was no longer alone in the room. At first Doreen didn't know whether to lie still and in fear with her eyes tightly closed or to open her eyes and see if her feeling was correct. Finally, with great force of will, she opened her eyes.

The colorless image of a man stood beside Doreen's bed. She knew instantly that he was not of this world.

"Go away," she urged, panicked by this supernatural scene. But the slightly transparent specter stayed exactly where he was. He was staring intently at Doreen and appeared to be speaking, although she could not hear any sound.

She closed her eyes, hoping to clear the image from her vision, but when she looked again, the ghost was even more obvious. This time she could see that he had a flower tightly gripped in the fist of his right hand. Slowly he moved his right arm until he seemed to be presenting the bloom to Doreen who stared back at the apparition, terrified.

His lips were still moving—over and over again they formed the same pattern. Although there was no sound and Doreen had no idea what it was he was saying, she could tell he was repeating the same declaration. Then his mouth was still for a moment, and the frightened woman was horrified to realize that the illusion was melting before her very eyes. Just before the ghost disappeared completely she clearly heard him say, "I've come to court you."

The ghost's intentions may have been sincere but his strength as a manifestation was not equal to the task, for he soon vanished completely. When Doreen mentioned the incident to her landlord the next morning, she was informed that over the years, this romantically inclined ghost had visited every single woman who had ever stayed in that particular room.

Free At Last

Cripple Creek, Colorado, lies west of Colorado Springs and southwest of Manitou Springs. From the 1860s to the early 1900s, the town was a typical gold-mining frontier settlement. Some of the buildings were constructed to last; others were simply shacks or tents. The streets of Cripple Creek may have been "paved" only with mud, but the surrounding hills were certainly filled with gold. It was a prosperous town. Even the devastating fires that twice leveled the entire town did not succeed in destroying the place. It took major labor disputes and the end of the gold to do that.

Even today, the spirit of the once-booming village remains. Cripple Creek is truly a ghost town with a living legacy—in the form of a large ghostly population from a long-ago era.

The Welty Block was one of Cripple Creek's historic haunts. This big old building housed a hotel, a restaurant, a grocery store, a Masonic hall and lots of ghosts. There were so many ghosts, in fact, that anyone working in the building soon learned that *para*normal activities were the norm. They simply learned to expect the unexpected.

When a family's pet dog, for instance, growled viciously at something no human could see, the people became resigned to the thought that the ghosts were about. When a couple's bed suddenly shook violently in the middle of the night, they wisely presumed a presence or two was there. When a veritable pageant of gorgeous, slightly transparent women walked by, everyone knew for certain that the phantoms had, once again, made their way back through the veil of time. And a worker who had done some carpentry in the building remembered being frustrated when his tools and equipment were frequently and mysteriously being moved around probably by a ghost.

The Welty Block would, without a doubt, still be very haunted had the place not burned to the ground on a freezing cold night early in March 1977.

Every firefighter for miles around was called out to help battle the flames, but despite their best, bone-chilling efforts, they lost both the fight and the historic building.

It was a distressing defeat, especially for a rookie firefighter who was sure someone had died in the blaze. Although he was told over and over again that the place had been completely empty at the time of the fire, he was never convinced that no lives had been lost. He always maintained that he had heard death cries.

Another man, a veteran on the pumper trucks, was also deeply disturbed by the fire. He, by coincidence, was the carpenter whose tools had mysteriously been moved around. As the Welty Block crashed down into a pile of burning rubble, this older man was sure that he heard a disembodied female screaming into the night. "I'm free! I'm free," the voice had apparently cackled.

At exactly the same moment, another man watched in awe as a perfectly formed image—the image of a woman—rose through the dense smoke and then disappeared into the night sky.

Spirits: Liquid and Vaporous

Percie Knowles routinely wanders about the Chico Hot Springs Resort in Pray, Montana. She's frequently seen walking about the place, supervising employees and generally keeping an eye on things. Percie's concern shouldn't really be surprising. As owner of the hotel, it's only reasonable that she would feel responsible for the place. The surprising part of her continuing involvement with the resort is that Percie Knowles has been dead since 1936. The woman's determination to have Chico Hot Springs Resort run her way has clearly continued well into her afterlife.

In 1900, Percie, her husband, Bill, and their two-year-old son, Radbourne, inherited property near the hot springs. Six months later they opened the doors to a hotel they had built on the land. Bill and Percie agreed to make the natural hot springs a focal point of their new investment, but they did not see eye to eye regarding serving alcohol at their hotel. Bill, who loved to drink and kibitz, insisted that the resort include a well-stocked bar. Percie wanted to offer a vacation spot with a resting and healing focus. Initially, Bill apparently won the argument because there was a bar on the premises until the day he died—in April 1910—of cirrhosis of the liver.

Bill's untimely death left Percie with a 12-year-old son to raise and a resort to run. Her first action as the new, sole owner was to close the bar. After hiring a physician, Dr. George A. Townsend, to live at Chico Springs in the resort, she began billing the hotel as a health care center. Percie's plan worked well, and she operated a highly successful spa until 1925 when Dr. Townsend retired and young

Radbourne left home to marry. Although she had a capable and loyal staff, the departure of her son and the physician left Percie with more responsibility than she wanted. The workload was too much for the woman. First her physical and then her mental health began to fail. Business declined and, in 1940, Percie Knowles died in a state-run medical facility. After her son died just three years later, the once-prosperous resort was abandoned and put up for sale.

John Sterhan, who owned the hotel from 1967 to 1972, was vague when asked about ghosts in the old place. He would acknowledge only that employees would occasionally report bizarre and inexplicable encounters. Sterhan sold the place to Mike and Eve Art, who worked hard to recapture the success that the inn had once enjoyed. Their efforts included renovations to the building, and, as such work has been known to turn latent spirits active, the ghostly activity became more intense.

Tim Barnes and Ron Woolery, two security guards at the hotel, had a supernatural experience there in the spring of 1986. It is unlikely that either of them will ever forget what occurred that night. Both men were familiar with the property and usually felt very comfortable with their duties. On this particular night, however, they were anything but comfortable. As they finished their duties, set the locks on the doors and prepared to leave, Barnes did a quick scan of the lobby. His eyes fell on something he'd never seen before—a gauzy, smoky formation roughly 5 feet (1.5 meters) above the floor. Within that blurry cloud was an upper body and a face—of a woman.

Woolery spun around when Barnes gasped involuntarily. Ron followed Tim's gaze, and seconds later he too was looking at the apparition. The ghost stared back at the men. They had both heard the rumors that the third floor of the resort was haunted, but neither had ever believed the tales. Now they were face to face with the rather convincing evidence.

Tim Barnes ran for a camera. He tried to snap a photograph of the manifestation, but either because he was unfamiliar with that camera or perhaps for more ethereal reasons, the exposure remained almost completely black. Less than a minute later the ghost herself disappeared. The men wasted no time leaving the building, but once they were outside they talked excitedly about their encounter. The most interesting part of their conversation was that while Tim was sure the specter they had seen was female, Ron was equally sure it had been male. They were never able to resolve their disagreement and even when the ghost is seen or felt today, some witnesses will report that it's female while others are sure it's male.

Tim Barnes' mother, Edie, who worked as the hotel's night auditor during the early 1990s, never doubted her son's word, for she also saw the ghost, which she described as being "cloudy and white, smoky and hazy but shaped like a person." The woman also agrees with her son that the ghost seemed to be female. Edie readily admitted that she was startled when she saw the spirit but indicated that the ghost also seemed to be startled. Presumably Edie looked as out of place in the spirit's world as the spirit did in Edie's.

That encounter at least prepared Edie for her second sighting of the vision. This time she was with another worker who agreed that the ghost was that of a woman.

It is interesting that when discussing these ghostly sightings some people use the pronoun "he" while others refer to the ghost as "she." This confusion is highly unusual and likely indicates that not only Percie's but also either Bill's or Radbourne's soul has remained at Chico Hot Springs.

Employees whose duties take them to the building's third floor like to stay away from room 349—the room where Percie Knowles lay ill before being taken to the hospital, as well as another room, one known to have been Bill Knowles' favorite. No one has ever reported seeing any images in either suite but almost all the workers who have entered those rooms say that they feel ill at ease until they leave. As well, footsteps are frequently heard along the third-floor hallway at times when any employees there can clearly see the corridor is deserted.

In other parts of the hotel, doors will slam closed for no apparent reason. Kitchen utensils will be rearranged in a locked and empty area. People have heard the sounds of someone preparing a meal in the kitchen, but when they check to see who could be making such a racket, the noises stop and they always find the room empty.

There is also a legend about Percie Knowles' Bible, which is stored in the hotel's attic. The place is no longer used so is generally quite dusty—except for the pages of Percie's Bible, which is always open and always, impossibly, dust free.

Larry Bohne, a security guard at the inn, may also have seen the ghost. He was patrolling the second-floor corridor of the empty building when he began to sense that he was no longer alone. Bohne looked up the staircase leading to the third floor and was very surprised to see an illusion looking down at him. He described her in detail—a middle-aged woman of average height wearing an old-fashioned dress. Larry was certain that this was not a person, though, because her face was "pale and without expression." Then, as she moved away, any doubts Larry might have had were effectively removed when she floated away before disappearing completely.

As he was in charge of security for the premises, Larry pursued the image. He found the building as empty as it should have been—except for the presence of a lingering aroma—a sweet smell that was strongest near room 349.

Others have also had encounters with Percie's ghost, and all their descriptions are amazingly similar. Charlie Wells, a security guard at the hotel from 1989 to 1990, saw a woman's image ascending the stairs. At first he thought it was actually a person but then he realized that the manifestation looked to be surrounded by a smoky haze. He also realized that the "person" he was staring at had on exactly the same dress as Percie Knowles did in a picture that hangs in the hotel lobby. He knew for certain that he'd seen the ghost.

Charlie was also sure that he saw the same presence, wearing the same clothes, sitting with a man in the dining room. When he checked more closely, he realized that there was no one in the room but that the two chairs he thought he'd seen the couple sitting in were pulled out as though they had just been used. That mystery was never solved.

At least one employee is sure that he saw only Bill Knowles and that he has never seen Percie. Bob Oppelt, who worked with Charlie Wells, indicated to author Debra Munn (in *Big Sky Ghosts*, Pruett Publishing, 1994) that he had watched in horror as an abnormally tall figure simply "appeared" in the corner of his room. The head of the image nearly touched the ceiling and when it began to walk, the movement was really more of a swaying motion. Although he was not able to make out the apparition's features, Oppelt was sure it was the ghost of a very tall man. Bob froze in fear and later reported that the room had become almost electrified with a decidedly eerie feeling. The frightened man escaped to the hallway and when he returned to his room, the image, but not the unpleasant atmosphere, was gone.

It took Bob Oppelt several days to get up the courage to speak of this encounter. When two other people said they'd seen a similar large figure, he felt his experience was validated.

The phantom can carry his or her pranks a bit too far on some occasions. For instance, the ghost has been blamed for files that disappear, only to reappear—on the back seat of a locked car. He or she has also been accused of taking money—not large amounts, though, just enough to cause an employee's bookkeeping to be out of balance. Phones occasionally ring when they shouldn't, and when those "calls" are answered, the person picking up the receiver can hear only a strange electrical hum on the line. Of course, this could be a result of non-ghostly activity, but when it happens immediately after an employee has detected some other form of ghostly activity, that possibility becomes less likely.

Perhaps it really isn't much of a surprise that Percie or Bill, or both of them, have never really left the resort they established. Lots of tourists, including the rich and famous, keep returning to the healing waters and warm hospitality. Of course, those folks are still alive. Who knows, the Knowles family may eventually have company in their afterlife at the hotel. Until then, they seem to be doing an excellent job on their own of haunting the Chico Hot Springs Resort.

Walter?

Hotels are unique establishments. They serve as temporary homes, occasionally during intensely emotional times. We stay in hotels not only during much-anticipated vacations but also during other trips that may be significant for happy or unhappy reasons. It's no wonder, then, that there are often strong feelings attached to these temporary residences. Some of those feelings, especially in historic hotels, apparently run so deep that even death cannot completely extinguish them.

While researching for the books of ghost stories I've written over the years, I've been intrigued by the different and sometimes changing attitudes of hoteliers toward their hauntings. Some Rocky Mountain hotels (the Banff Springs Hotel in Banff, Alberta, is an excellent example) once acknowledged and even embraced the ghostly legends that had become connected with their hotel over the years. Then, perhaps spurred by a change in either management or clientele, the official policy of some of those hotels simply became one of denial.

When I mentioned this to a former employee of the Banff Springs Hotel, he mused, "I wonder what they've done with all the ghosts, then." Other inns, the Hotel Colorado being one, don't go so far as to deny the existence of their resident ghosts, but no longer promote their ghost stories. Be that as it may, the Colorado has a long, proud and haunted heritage.

The Hotel Colorado is located at the confluence of the Colorado and Roaring Fork rivers in Glenwood Springs, Colorado. The "Springs" in the community's name refers to natural springs on the hotel's property that have long been thought to have healing properties. Partly for those curative powers, the hotel has attracted rich, famous and powerful guests since the day it opened in 1893.

The Colorado was also the birthplace of the teddy bear. In 1905, President Theodore (Teddy) Roosevelt stayed at the hotel while on a bear-hunting expedition. When he returned from a hard day's hunt with no trophy to show for his efforts, some of the staff at the Hotel Colorado fashioned a small bear out of leftover pieces of cloth and presented it to the president as a token of consolation for his disappointment. A member of the local press heard about this whimsical act of kindness and wrote about it in his newspaper. The scribe referred to the unnamed gift as a "Teddy Bear." A new toy was born, and teddy bears have been central to the luxurious hotel ever since. The ghosts in residence have also been a focal point.

Some debate exists over who the cigar-smoking ghost roaming about the Hotel Colorado might have been when he was alive. The manifestation might be that of E.E. Lucas, who began working at the hotel in 1893. Lucas loved the grand inn and at the time of his death in 1927, he actually owned the place. For this reason, some people think that his spirit is keeping a spectral eye on the place he was so attached to during his lifetime. Other people maintain that the ghost is that of Hervey Lyle, who was also closely involved with the Hotel Colorado. Still others are sure the spirit is that of Walter Devereux, the builder and first owner of the luxurious hotel.

Despite that difference of opinion, the ghost has responded to the name "Walter" when chastised for interfering with work and by now is routinely referred to as Walter. Whoever this ghost is, or was when he was alive, there seems to be no question of his presence throughout the hotel. Many employees attest that they have felt a male presence with them and that they have smelled cigar smoke during one or more of their shifts when there was no one—male or female, with or without a cigar—anywhere near them.

In 1994, a manager named Chuck, who lived at the hotel, had an unnerving and possibly supernatural experience. He was alone in his room relaxing, watching television after work one day when he began the feel that there was someone in the room with him. At first Chuck tried to disregard the uncomfortable sensation, but he found this increasingly difficult, especially once his television set started flipping from one channel to another and the smell of phantom cigar smoke became thick in the air.

A guest staying in that same room sometime after Chuck's experience did not smell any smoke, but she did have a strange experience. After closing the windows, tidying the place up a bit and having a shower, the woman came back into the main room to find the window open and her books on the floor. Again she closed the windows and tidied up before returning to the bathroom to dry her hair. Ten minutes later her hair was dry, the windows were wide open again and the books were back on the floor. She was the only one in the room at that time, and the door had been securely locked.

While that strange experience might not have involved Walter, his spirit has actually been seen and identified. He often sits in a chair near the hotel's front door. He never disturbs anyone but just sits there smoking his cigar. Anyone who's seen the ghost knows it is an apparition and not a being from this world because he appears only briefly and is dressed in clothing from a bygone era.

Though seeing a ghost is rare and capturing such an image on film is even more unusual, it is believed that Walter's likeness may have shown up in a publicity photograph taken by a professional photographer a few years ago inside the hotel. The unusual frame was one of a series of shots. The ghostly image is evident only in that one exposure.

According to reports, Walter does not always stay in the building or even on its grounds. A secretary named Patti at the Hotel Colorado believes that Walter may have accompanied her home one night when she needed a little extra help. The woman was extremely tired that evening, perhaps too tired to have been driving safely. As she wearily drove along the highway, she suddenly smelled cigar smoke in the car. Because she was alone, and certainly not smoking a cigar, the aroma gave her quite a start—enough of a start to snap her out of her sleepiness and make her pay more attention to the road.

Walter demonstrates just as much concern for the hotel itself as he does for its employees. When doors inside the building swing open and elevators operate with no one near them, today's employees just presume it's Walter keeping an eye on the place.

Whoever he is, Devereux, Lucas or Lyle, this spirit definitely wants to be acknowledged. Strange things have happened concerning the candles in the hotel's dining room. One candle, for instance, could burn for hours and hours—longer than it should have been able to—while the flame on another might appear to be reacting to a brisk draft when there is none. Occasionally, one or more of the candles simply cannot be lit. No reason for any of these anomalies has ever been found, but, partly because the dining room is called the Devereux Room, the inexplicable occurrences are generally credited to, or blamed on, Walter.

In keeping with standard ghostly practices, phones throughout the hotel have also been known to ring randomly when no one is on the line. One time this annoying activity continued for 12 hours straight despite skilled workers' attempts to stop the nuisance.

Phantom smells are often present in a haunted building, and there are certainly many different aromas at the Hotel Colorado. A chef who lived in a private residence on the property frequently smelled perfume in his suite when there was no reason for such a scent. This fragrance may have indicated the presence of a spirit named Roberta.

During her lifetime, "Bobbie," as the manifestation is commonly called, favored a certain perfume called Gardenia. Interestingly, research bears out the accuracy of this connection. Roberta had been a nurse in residence at the hotel during the Second World War. Her signature fragrance was new and very popular in that era, but it hasn't been manufactured for many decades now.

Bobbie's lingering presence has been detected by both employees and patrons. She's most often detected while Sunday brunch is being served at the hotel. Once a worker followed the distinctive fragrance of the ghost's perfume as it moved out of the dining room and across to the hotel's reception desk before fading away.

Perhaps the strangest report of the phantom smell occurred while an employee was on top of a ladder. He was hanging festive decorations above the lobby area when he recognized the aroma. When he came down the ladder, he could no longer smell the perfume, but when another employee climbed up the ladder she could also smell it. Perhaps Bobbie had taken advantage of her weightlessness and had floated up to see what the man was working on.

If that is so, then it might have been Bobbie who, every so often, caused the heavy chandeliers suspended from the ceiling in the lobby to swing about as though someone was pushing them. And it also might have been Bobbie who, several times, called out a pleasant "hello" to a maintenance man. No other person—man or woman—was anywhere near him when the man heard the voice greeting him.

When a former resident of the hotel returned for a visit, she began telling an employee about the female apparition she and others had been aware of years before. Even as she related these 30-year-old events, strange activities—those commonly associated with the presence of a ghost—began to happen around her. First the television turned on although there was no one near it; then as the door to the room opened by itself, the television began to change channels as the bewildered witnesses stood 10 feet (3 meters) from it.

Bobbie may or may not be the specter that many hotel guests over the years have reported seeing in and around their rooms. This image wears a floral dress and demonstrates a decidedly caring nature. In 1993, a couple booked into one of the bell tower suites. The man was feeling ill when he and his wife first arrived at the hotel. As a result, he spent the first few days of their visit resting in their luxurious rooms.

Thinking that the fresh mountain air would help her husband feel better, the woman made sure the windows in the suite were always open. After seeing that the rooms were ventilated in that way and that her husband was comfortable, she would often leave the sixth floor suite briefly to enjoy the hotel's grounds. Moments after she left, another woman appeared in the room. The ailing man could not identify the figure that appeared but watched as the ghost promptly closed all the windows his wife had just opened. Before disappearing, the apparition explained her actions to the man by telling him, "You need to stay out of the draft." Fortunately, in spite of those caring but conflicting actions, the man was well again after three days.

Mirrors have long been associated with the supernatural, and mirrors in hotels can be especially disturbing.

Marilyn Monroe's image, for instance, is said to appear in a prominently placed mirror at the Roosevelt Hotel in Hollywood, California. That mirror once stood in Miss Monroe's favorite suite at the Roosevelt (see my *Ghost Stories of Hollywood,* Lone Pine Publishing, 2000).

The Hotel Colorado had an equally strange mirror. The edges of this mirror were always cool to the touch while the center of the surface seemed to radiate heat. On one occasion, two employees discovered that if they laid their hands on the reflecting glass, a black smoking hole formed in the mirror. No explanation has ever been found for that eerie phenomenon.

In 1982, a ghostly decorator visited another room. Workers had spent most of the day hanging wallpaper in a fifth-floor suite. The next day they were extremely disturbed to find every piece of the paper off the wall and on the floor. Not knowing what else to do, the workers simply redid the project. The following morning they arrived to find that, again, their effort had been for nothing—the paper was all off the walls and back down on the floor. Realizing that they were working in a haunted hotel, the paper-hangers decided not to fight this unseen force any further but to try to cooperate with it. They chose three different selections of wallpaper and laid a roll of each out on the bed in the room. The next morning two rolls were on the floor and only one remained on the bed. They dispensed with the rolls on the floor and hung the paper that was still on the bed. The wallpaper has stayed on those walls ever since.

A psychic visiting the hotel from the British Isles heard about this bizarre event. She apparently detected the spirit of one of the men who had helped to build the hotel. She felt his presence near the room with all the strange wallpaper activity, so perhaps it was his spirit that successfully influenced the workers' selection.

Over the years many children have stayed at the hotel. Some of them—their spirits anyway—have never left. A few years ago a woman was enjoying a visit to the Hotel Colorado with her grandson. One day, when she was looking for the youngster, she saw a little boy at the end of a hallway. Presuming it was her grandson, she walked toward him. As she did, the image vanished before her eyes. Her grandson had been nowhere near that hallway at that time.

The manifestation of a little girl who, legend has it, died at the hotel as a result of a fall, is also frequently seen. She is dressed in Victorian clothing and has even been known to play with the flesh-and-blood children vacationing at the Colorado.

Less detailed reports of other spirits throughout the extraordinary inn include the manifestation of an elderly woman in the laundry room and a cowboy dressed in gear from the 1800s who disappears when approached.

These are just some of the ghost stories from the Hotel Colorado. With a phantom population this large, perhaps the owners no longer promote interest in the hauntings simply to keep life just a little less complicated.

Wilson Awaits

Lake Louise, in the Canadian Rockies, is the largest and most beautiful lake in Banff National Park. The first explorer to set eyes on the lake's distinctive turquoise waters was Tom Wilson, who came across the area in 1882 and for obvious reasons named it Emerald Lake.

By 1890 the Canadian Pacific Railway had built the first hotel on the shores of the lake that, by then, had been renamed Lake Louise, in honor of Queen Victoria's fourth daughter. Despite the possible slight implied by the name change, Wilson never lost his love for the place. He returned to visit the area frequently and always stayed at the newly constructed Chateau Lake Louise. He loved to stroll about the hotel's rooftop walkway and admire the breathtaking view of the lake.

Some years later the CPR enlarged the hotel to include a second-story dining room. Wilson's walkway was sacrificed to make way for the addition, but out of respect for the explorer the room was named the Tom Wilson Room.

Apparently neither Wilson's death nor the destruction of his walkway could stop the man from enjoying the view he so loved. His ghostly image has been seen standing, staring out a window at the pristine view of the lake. There's never any question that the specter is that of Tom Wilson. He is seen only at Wilson's favorite vantage point and he's also recognized—by his "well-worn felt hat" and "distinctive leathery face."

One other well-known specter at the Chateau Lake Louise is generally believed to have already been haunting the place in 1924 when a destructive fire broke out.

The ghost of Rockies explorer Tom Wilson returns to enjoy his favorite view of Lake Louise in Alberta.

Some believe that the ghost not only caused the fire but then ran outside and had his ghostly image captured and preserved in a photograph. We can only hope that these two ghosts, one who always loved the hotel and one who allegedly damaged it, are not aware of one another's presence in the hotel.

Millie's Place

The exact location of this haunted mountain hostelry must remain a mystery. For our purposes here we will only state that it is located in a small town in the mountains of Colorado. Unfortunately, we must leave the location vague, for the hotel still stands and the current owners absolutely deny the veracity of the ghost stories. Out of respect for these people and their opinion, we shall not even give the name of the hotel but simply call it "Millie's Place" in honor of the spirit said to haunt the place.

Fortunately, the details of this haunting are not nearly as obscure as its identity must be. Reports of the paranormal activity have been well documented over the years and are extremely specific. Presuming that the ghostly legends surrounding the hotel are accurate, this is a very long-standing haunting. Paranormal activities at the inn were first reported in the late 1860s, just after the Civil War.

The descriptions of the ghost, and of visitors' encounters with her, are all remarkably alike. Invariably, guests who are going to have any sort of ghostly experience in the hotel will have their first exposure to the phantom very soon after checking in. As they make their way along one of the three hallways in the hotel, a little girl will approach the tourists and ask if they have seen her mother. When the people go to get help for the little girl, she disappears, because she was never really there in the first place—it was only her image from the afterlife that they saw and heard.

The little waif's name is Millie. Her father was the hotel manager, and she lived with her parents at the hotel until her mother's death from tuberculosis when the little girl was only five years old. The child was never able to accept her mother's death and spent the rest of her own short life being absolutely sure that her mother was still somewhere in the building. The child continually wandered the hotel's hallways asking people she saw if they'd seen her mother. Late one night when the corridors and staircases were in darkness and Millie was searching for her beloved mother, the little girl fell down the stairs—to her death.

The child's body was buried in one of the eastern states, but her soul stayed in the hotel, still determined to find her mother.

Unlike many other ghosts, Millie seems aware of the existence of the living. When a chambermaid saw the child's image, she was sure it really was a little girl. The specter was solid and in no way gave the impression of being anything other than a human being. Furthermore, when the maid smiled at the little girl, Millie smiled back at her. The maid thought nothing of the experience until later in the day when she was talking to another member of the cleaning staff. That woman reported having seen the same child, wearing the same clothes, at the same time but in a different location. As the two women tried to sort out what might have caused this enigma, one of them looked up to a photograph that hung on the hotel wall. It was a picture of Millie Pratt. Both women agreed that this was the child they had seen.

Not everyone who encounters Millie actually sees her. Some witnesses just feel pockets of cold air randomly throughout the hotel. These are not normally chilly places—the pockets of cold air move around the hotel and are never in the same place again. Other people have reported hearing the ghostly girl's little feet skipping along the hallways. Still others will suddenly become aware of a flowery scent in the room with them. This light fragrance does not lead to any further paranormal activity. Usually, the aroma simply disappears shortly after it has arrived.

Other people say that they have heard a ghostly echo of the fatal fall that Millie took down the stairs. Not surprisingly those witnesses say the phantom sounds of the little body hitting one stair after another are gruesome and unsettling to hear.

In the late 1970s a couple who had checked into the hotel were both overcome with sadness as soon as they settled into their room. They were on a holiday that they'd looked forward to for many years so were surprised by the melancholy feelings. The pair decided to turn in early in the hope of sleeping off the unpleasant sensation. Just as they were drifting off to sleep they could hear clothes in the closet of their room being moved about. Seconds later the woman distinctly heard a child's voice call out "Mommy?"

The woman jumped from the bed. She was sure a child was trapped in their room. She and her husband turned on all the lights in the room and searched thoroughly but could not find anything. Finally, they gave up the hunt and went back to bed. As soon as they did the little girl began calling for her mother again. This time the woman decided that they must get help, and she ran out of the room and down the hallway. She could hear the sounds of someone very small, the size of a little girl, skipping along beside her. Those sounds ended as soon as they reached the staircase. The woman will never forget what happened next: as she put her foot down onto the top step she heard, but could not see, the sounds of a child falling down to the very bottom of the stairs. Then, all was silent.

Millie's is not the only ghost rumored to be at this Rocky Mountain resort. At different times several men who were staying at the hotel have sworn that they have seen the apparition of a Civil War soldier in their room. As Millie's father fought in that war, it may be his soul that has returned to the hotel he ran.

In a last sad, ironic note, it must be said that no one, not even Millie's ghost, has ever seen her mother's image.

Miss Kate Presides Here

The Sheridan Inn is "a symbol of the people who believed in America, believed enough to move west to create a life in the wilderness. They, their spirit, built this inn…" So said Neltje Kings, former owner of the Sheridan, Wyoming, hostelry, in 1965. Almost 40 years later, it could also be said that at least some of those spirits have never left the inn they built.

It was the spring of 1893 when the Sheridan Inn, with its multi-gabled roof, first greeted guests. In those early days Buffalo Bill Cody leased the inside of the building and even used the inn's huge veranda as an audition hall for performers wanting to join his Wild West show. Over the years, presidents, artists, actors and authors have enjoyed staying in the impressive old building. Ernest Hemingway was living at the inn in the 1920s when he began writing his classic World War I novel, *A Farewell To Arms*.

The hotel attracted not only extraordinary guests but also extraordinary workers and business associates—beginning, of course, with Buffalo Bill Cody. In 1901, while Cody was still involved with the inn, a 22-year-old woman named Kate Arnold arrived in Sheridan looking for work. She found the employment she was seeking, initially as a seamstress at the hotel. Miss Kate, as she was always known, remained with the inn for the next 64 years, even when ownership changed hands. Her association with the hotel would no doubt have continued until her death had the property not been sold to a company determined to demolish the building.

With luck and a lot of hard work by community-minded citizens, the historic Sheridan Inn was saved from demolition, so when Kate died three years later, her spirit was able to return to the only home she'd ever known as an adult. To date, her essence has still not left.

Miss Kate's ghost is a benign presence, but she has been known to startle a few unsuspecting folks.

George Carmichael, a pianist working at the inn, is an excellent example of just such an individual. One beautiful spring morning in 1970 Carmichael woke to find that he was not alone. Over by the window was a tiny woman wearing an old-fashioned, long, light blue dress. Carmichael was not frightened by the presence, for it was so real looking that it never crossed his mind that this was anything other than a flesh-and-blood person.

He called out to her, asking if she needed any help, but what he really wanted to ask her was how she had been able to get into his room when he knew that his door had been locked all night. When the figure seemed to ignore him, George Carmichael spoke again. This time the woman turned her head and looked directly at him before vanishing completely. Carmichael was flabbergasted. It's a good thing that he wasn't aware at the time that this ghost was known to sit on people's beds and, after disappearing, leave a clear indentation where she'd sat on the bed.

After Carmichael had composed himself, he dressed and went downstairs to talk to the workers in the Sheridan Inn's kitchen. As calmly as possible, Carmichael told the others about his recent encounter. The cooks were not surprised to hear what he had to say. It wasn't that they knew the pianist was given to flights of fancy—on the contrary, they knew he was a down-to-earth person. They also knew that the Sheridan Inn was haunted by the ghost of Miss Kate Arnold.

These folks were used to the spirit's antics. They would routinely have to reset tables when their cutlery and plates mysteriously went missing. But they weren't the only ones associated with the place who were convinced that the building was haunted. There's not much point in doubting the ghost's existence in the historic building because, in death, Miss Kate's body was actually brought back and her cremated remains were laid to rest inside the walls of the room that had been hers for over 60 years. Today the woman's manifestation is seen as the hotel's guardian.

According to promotional material issued by the group that currently manages the inn, those who have worked on the hotel's restoration become aware of Miss Kate, as her "presence is felt on an almost daily basis." She's credited with "turning lights off and on, [with] opening and closing doors" and generally making sure that everyone is well aware that she has not left the building and is still a force to be reckoned with when the old inn is concerned.

The ghost seems to be aware that the people who are in "her" hotel today are merely trying to preserve this important piece of history, but when those folks impose a change not to her liking, she's swift to deliver her opinion. When the old Buffalo Bill Bar, for instance, was turned into a venue for rock music performances, the ghost succeeded very dramatically in making her displeasure known. All the musicians complained that their usually reliable instruments would simply not stay in tune. One man maintained that his guitar had fallen from its stand with enough force that it broke.

The ghost has also been credited with causing a bottle from the bar to lift off its shelf and crash into a wall at the back of the room. To any skeptics out there who think that a patron of the lounge perhaps threw the bottle: be advised that everyone in the bar was drinking beer in cans. No one in the place was holding a bottle of any thing, much less a bottle from behind the bar.

Probably the most annoying trick Miss Kate's phantom put over on the musicians, though, was to make strange sounds come out of the bands' amplifiers and ruin their performances.

A long-term employee at the inn declared simply, and seemingly accurately, "Miss Kate doesn't like rock music."

She was fond of the original equipment from the hotel's glory days and used two of the old cash registers to very emphatically inform a particularly skeptical employee of her continuing existence at the inn. A group of workers were discussing the haunting when their superior informed them that they were being silly. The words were no sooner out of the woman's mouth than two of the preserved antique cash registers began working. There was no one anywhere near them at the time.

A landscaper employed at the Sheridan Inn apparently had a long relationship with the resident ghost. The specter would sit on his bed and tell him of her concerns about the work that was going on at the inn. Then, when she'd made her thoughts known, she'd get up from his bed, leaving an impression of where she'd sat, walk out of the room into the hallway and simply disappear

172 Ghost Stories of the Rocky Mountains, Volume II

into the darkness. When her stated wishes were not respected, Miss Kate's spirit became more forthright, moving pieces of furniture or draperies back to where they'd always been—and where she evidently wanted them to stay.

Once, in a direct attempt to appease the woman's spirit, the manager at that time placed a pretty vase filled with silk flowers in the room where Kate Arnold's ashes are interred. This ploy worked for a while until a certain change was made in the hotel's furnishing. When this happened, the vase, with its flowers, would routinely be found knocked over, although no one had been in or out of the locked room. No one human, that is.

That vase containing one silk flower is still in that room, as are other objects that Miss Kate owned in her life. The room and everything in it is dusty—except the flower. It, impossibly, stays free of dust all the time.

If you get the chance to drop in to the historic Sheridan Inn, do. It is a beautiful spot. And when you're touring the ballroom area of the old hotel there's no need to be frightened when the curtains in the huge room lift ever so slightly. That'll just be the ghost of Miss Kate Arnold continuing to check on the building she devoted her life—and now devotes her afterlife—to preserving.

Neljte would no doubt be pleased.

4
Snippets

Sometimes only fragments of ghost stories remain to scare us. Sometimes, however, those fragments can be even more provocative than a complete anecdote.

Now Grandma's Gone

When Kathryn O'C (her name has been shortened here to protect her anonymity) was a student in Helena, Montana, she enjoyed an especially close relationship with her grandmother. The girl would often know intuitively that her grandmother was about to call, and when she did call it was frequently to invite Kathryn to join her on some sort of an outing.

After Kathryn's grandmother died, the woman's spirit returned—to her beloved granddaughter, of course—to assure the youngster that the passage from life to the afterlife was "not as bad as" she'd thought it was going to be.

For days after that first visit, Kathryn would wake up to sense a presence in her bedroom. If the girl opened her eyes at those times, she would see an illuminated orb of light floating about her bedroom. Although Kathryn was comforted by her grandmother's presence, she was also concerned that the older woman's soul might become stranded on earth rather than making its way to the great beyond. Courageously and selflessly, the young woman urged her grandmother's soul to continue on its journey. Apparently, the woman's ghost followed her granddaughter's suggestion because Kathryn has never seen or felt any trace of the spirit since that time.

Lifesaver

Malcolm, it seemed, was born to ranch. Fortunately, he was also born on a ranch. Even before he ever attended kindergarten, the boy routinely helped herd the family's cattle. The little boy knew horses, he knew cattle and he knew his family's land. His father had taught him that if he ever became separated from the others during a roundup he was to head for the creek and follow it to his uncle's place.

Then, one day, Malcolm did become isolated from the other riders. Worse, he knew he was in bear country and that he was completely alone. He rode here and there, back and forth, trying to find his way and fight panic as the sun fell to the west. Just as it was starting to get fully dark out, a man rode up to the child and quietly guided him safely home.

The family was as happy to see the little boy as they were relieved. When he turned to thank his rescuer, though, Malcolm could hardly believe his eyes. There was no sign of either the man or his horse.

"What did the man look like?" the adults prompted the child. "If you describe him we'll know who it is and know who we should thank."

The child described a tall man with long black hair, a mustache and sparkling blue eyes astride a dapple gray horse named Gray Eagle. Malcolm had perfectly described his grandfather—who had been dead for many years before the little boy had been born. His ghost, however, had evidently returned to keep his grandson safe.

Wandering for Eternity

We no longer know when John Baptiste lived, and no one (except Baptiste himself, of course) ever knew when he died. We do know that John Baptiste is still roaming the north shores of Utah's Great Salt Lake.

When he was alive, Baptiste lived in a tiny shack at the corner of K Street and South Temple in Salt Lake City. He earned his living as a well-respected gravedigger. It was eventually discovered that he supplemented his wages with a related sideline—that of grave robber.

The man's part-time "job" might have gone unnoticed for years except that, for undisclosed reasons, a particular family decided to have a deceased relative disinterred. When the coffin was opened those in attendance were shocked to find that the body had been stripped of every bit of clothing and had been unceremoniously dumped back into the box facedown.

When word of this horror leaked out, other families came forward to ask that the graves of their loved ones be reopened. The community was horrified to discover that this sacrilege had been wrought upon almost every corpse in the field.

The authorities immediately set out to arrest John Baptiste. He was found not long after, pushing a wheelbarrow full of clothing toward his two-room dwelling. After waiting a few minutes until Baptiste had time to settle in for the night, the police banged on his door. Without waiting for the courtesy of an invitation, they barged into the tiny place. What they found in the home confirmed for them that he was definitely not only the local gravedigger but also the local grave robber.

Baptiste was arrested then and there. After due process he was charged and sentenced to exile on an island in the Salt Lake.

Less than a month later authorities rowed out to the island to check on the prisoner. They found the remnants of a crude shelter and the remains of a fire pit but John Baptiste himself was nowhere to be found. The guards were surprised as well as angered that this man who'd committed such a heinous crime had escaped. They searched for their convict on other islands, they searched for signs of a raft and they searched for a body. They found nothing and to date nothing is known for certain of the details of John Baptiste's demise.

A few months later, people began to share stories about a man they'd seen walking along the shore of the lake. As more and more folks saw the image they became bolder and bolder. Determined to discover who this stranger was, one after another, they tried to approach him. Without exception, the presence vanished before they were close enough to call out to him.

But isn't it too much of a stretch to assume from these bits of information that the man walking on the beach was actually the ghost of John Baptiste? Perhaps, except that everyone who has seen the nighttime walker has reported that he is easy to recognize—by the pile of dirty old clothing he carries into eternity.

Ghost Rider

Groups of early settlers often sent riders ahead to determine which route would be the safest and easiest to continue on. Not all of those scouts returned. Some met their demise shortly after heading out. A few of those unfortunate souls, like the one who haunts the hills near Cheyenne, Wyoming, seem damned to continue their patrol forever.

On clear nights when there is a full moon, this ghostly rider and his steed can be seen galloping over the land. People who've seen the sight have been shocked at the speed at which the rider and horse were traveling. Thinking that the man is panicked and must be in need of assistance, many have ridden out to offer help.

Those who attempted to extend such kindness have reported that the dark image did not slow upon approach but barreled past them as though they were not even there. The apparition is soundless, but it leaves a residue of icy coldness behind it. Witnesses say their horses reacted violently to this encounter by rearing and bucking—apparently terrified by the unnatural sight.

Perhaps if you want to enjoy a late-night ride near Cheyenne you'd do best to pick a cloudy night at a time when there will not be a full moon—unless, that is, you want to see a ghost!

Dread 107

There are some trains that no one should ever try to catch. "Dread 107" was definitely one of those. Too many times, after leaving its roundhouse in Grand Junction, Colorado, locomotive 107 derailed. Over the years, the list of 107's victims grew until finally in 1909, the cumbersome piece of machinery was retired in a hopeful attempt to set its grisly legacy to rest.

Strange then, isn't it, that the image of the enormous engine continues to be seen? It is an easily recognizable image of the long-retired engine 107. But the locomotive is not real and hasn't been for nearly a century. It is a phantom.

The apparition is easy to identify because it is an old-fashioned steam engine. The phantom of locomotive 107, now known as Dread 107, chugs along into eternity on nonexistent tracks—before the eyes of believers and disbelievers both.

Death Foretold

The following is not truly a ghost story. It is, though, one of the most intriguing supernatural tales ever reported.

By now, no one knows exactly where within the Rocky Mountains this incident occurred, but fortunately most of the other details have been preserved.

In 1862, a man named Carpenter was newly married. He adored his bride and wanted to provide her with the best, so he set out to make his fortune by joining thousands of others in the search for gold.

The journey was tremendously difficult, both mentally and physically. For the first week of the trek, Carpenter was horrified each time he passed corpses of those who had died along the trail, those who had already tried—and failed—to get to the riches ahead of him. Gradually, though, like the others in the long human chain of fortune seekers, he became hardened against the morbid reality. It was the loneliness for his beloved wife that the man was never able to tolerate.

As his group of hopeful miners approached a body of water that was particularly dangerous looking, Carpenter insisted on stopping. "I can't go on just yet," he explained to the man behind him before standing to the side of the path and scratching some words onto a scrap of paper. Carpenter stuffed the note he had just written into his coat pocket before hanging the garment on a nearby tree limb and setting out to cross the current.

Seconds later, the man was swept away by the roiling waters. When his friends found Carpenter's lifeless body not far downstream, they hauled it up onto the shore.

The men agreed to leave the body there, and then they continued on their quest. All, that is, except the man who had been walking directly behind the deceased. That man decided to pay Carpenter a final courtesy by covering his body with the coat he had abandoned just before stepping into the river. As the man pulled Carpenter's coat down from the limb, a small piece of paper fluttered to the ground. Curious, the man picked it up. It was a note—the note that Carpenter had stopped to write before wading to his death. The man read the words before him with disbelief.

"Arrived this day at the canyon at 10 AM and drowned. God keep my poor wife."

How Carpenter could have known about his impending death will always be a mystery—an intriguing supernatural mystery.

Butch Cassidy

It has been proposed that the more colorful someone's personality is in this life, the more likely he or she will have the aural strength to return after death. Often it does seem that people who are larger than life are those who come back to haunt us after they are gone. This is certainly the case in the following short but true story.

For years, Butch Cassidy, the Sundance Kid and a gang of bandits known as the Wild Bunch roamed the West, wreaking havoc wherever they went. They robbed banks, jumped trains to relieve the companies of any payrolls they might be carrying, hid out and served time in jail. These men, especially their leaders Butch and Sundance, were not mild-mannered individuals by any means. They were big, bold characters.

In 1896, Cassidy walked out of the Wyoming Penitentiary a free man. While he'd been serving time, many members of the Wild Bunch had gone straight. They had built themselves shacks that passed for homesteads and, to the best of their ability, settled down.

During the first few days of his newfound freedom, Cassidy thought he might join his friends who were enjoying a law-abiding life. He built himself a cabin in Brown's Park, Colorado, and resolved to retire from life as an outlaw. Butch Cassidy's resolve did not last long, for he soon found that theft was a much easier way to make money. And although the circumstances and location of his final demise have always been unclear, we do know that when he died he was on the run from the law.

Did two wranglers encounter the ghost of Butch Cassidy at his Colorado hideaway, long since collapsed?

Wherever and whenever the famed outlaw died, his spirit apparently returned to that cabin in northwestern Colorado. When the dilapidated old cabin still stood, a pair of wranglers stopped there to rest for a while. As they approached the small building, they saw a man standing in the doorway. Thinking that they should introduce themselves to the property owner, the two approached the place. As they did, the image vanished. They searched throughout the little house but no one was anywhere to be seen, and there were no signs that anyone had even been near the place for years.

Later the two men discovered that the cabin they had stopped at was, in fact, the very one built by Butch Cassidy. They also discovered that it was the man's habit to go to the door whenever he heard the sounds of horses' hooves approaching. They knew then and there that they had seen the ghost of Butch Cassidy. Definitely a story for the men's grandchildren to hear!

Haunted Hotel

There was a hospital in Virginia City, Montana, during the 1800s where many people died, some from excruciatingly painful wounds and illnesses. Later, when the hospital was no longer required, the building was purchased and renovated to become a hotel. It seems that many of the patients, though, had not left. Guests used to complain of apparitions walking the floors with bandaged limbs and of hearing moans and groans of agony through the night when they were trying to sleep. Perhaps it is not much of a surprise that the transformation from a place to care for the sick and dying to a place to welcome healthy, paying guests was not a success. The haunted building that was first a hospital and then a hotel has been closed for years now. Hopefully those souls who were suffering into their eternity have gone on to a peaceful and comfortable afterlife.

Monk's Manifestation

The "gold in them thar hills" attracted a lot of eccentrics to the Rockies. It also created a few. People who left their homes in the East filled with confidence, optimism and sanity were often short on all three after a few years of trying to get their share of the riches.

We don't know whether the man who came to be called the Bulgarian Monk was in possession of all his faculties when he reached the Salmon River in southwestern Idaho. We do know that by the time of his premature death, he was a very odd and extremely recognizable character.

The Bulgarian Monk dressed in robes and wore an odd little hat. He gave the impression that he was a missionary and claimed that he could speak 32 languages (although no one remembers him speaking anything other than English). "I guided Mark Twain through Jerusalem," he would often tell people as he spoke to them in passing. He was certainly not unfriendly but was never known to have sought out company. His aging dog and two tired-looking horses were with him at all times. No one knew exactly where the Monk lived, but those same folks knew all the odd man's favorite spots for hunting and fishing. Certainly no one feared him, but it is equally certain that no one loved him.

During the winter of 1890, the weather was so severe that many people died. Some were suffocated under tons of snow after avalanches rolled mercilessly down the mountainsides. Others froze to death after being stranded too long by the cold and snow. And it was during that winter that the Bulgarian Monk disappeared.

As winter turned to spring, several children reported having seen the strange man. They told the adults in their village that the Monk had played with them at the side of the riverbank before jumping into the water and vanishing. One of the people listening to the children's tale was especially distressed by their words because he knew that he had seen the Monk in town, some miles away, at the same time the children said the man was with them.

That coincidence left all the community members puzzled—until seeing the Bulgarian Monk, or more correctly, seeing the ghost of the Bulgarian Monk, became common place. His image, with robes flowing, was apparently often seen along the riverbank.

It's been years now since anyone has reported seeing the ghostly Monk. Hopefully, the odd man, his horses and his dog are by now together and enjoying their afterlives.

Haunting Avoided

Cemeteries are significant places in every culture, but as Native Americans believe that a person's spirit remains on earth until their bones disintegrate, burial grounds are especially revered within their society. It is important, they believe, not to disturb a person's remains for fear of disturbing that person's soul, causing the deceased to haunt either the person or the place.

Just east of the very haunted land where the Battle of Little Bighorn was fought in 1876 (see my *Ghost Stories of the Rocky Mountains*, Lone Pine Publishing, 1999) is another area where ancient spirits were thought to roam. Unfortunately, progress dictated that by 1987 a road had to be constructed through exactly that same area. As the roadwork began, the workers came across the grave of a child. The crew's foreman immediately shut the job site down and called Bill Tall Bull, a highly respected elder from a nearby community.

Tall Bull knew that if he didn't disinter the body it would forever be lying under traffic, which would not be acceptable. But he didn't want to move the remains from their resting place. He asked the spirits for guidance with his dilemma and, over time, was instructed as to where and how the body should be placed. Oddly, the directions he received were that the little body should be placed on its side facing west. Bill did has he'd been directed, although he had never heard of any group of people having such a burial custom.

Bill Tall Bull must have followed his orders from the other world properly, for the child's soul continued to rest in peace and the modern roadway was completed without a hitch. When relating the incident, however, Bill Tall Bull did add the caution for all of us that we must respect the earth and all that is part of it.

Stan's Spirit

A house in Butte, Montana, is haunted by a ghost named Stan who seems to have a particular dislike for electronic equipment. The two women who lived in this house were known as especially practical. Their friends were all the more confused, therefore, when the roommates told them about putting compact discs in the stereo and never being able to get them out again. A few weeks later the tenants swore that videotapes placed in the VCR would shoot out of the machine with such force that they would land across the room.

Even the television set and telephone malfunctioned, but only at times when the homeowners felt the supernatural presence was near. Sometimes the phone would ring when there was no one on the line. Often when the friends were enjoying a television show, the channel would simply change.

The pair became very used to their strange living conditions although they did say that it would've been nice to have been able to watch a movie in their house without fearing that they would be hit by a flying video!

Lesson Well Learned

The foothills area near the Wyoming-Montana border has changed very little over the years. Just as it is today, 30 years ago it was an idyllic place for a boy to roam, and that is just exactly what John Young loved to do. Sometimes he would find arrowheads or other tools used by the Native Indian peoples who once lived in the mountains. He would pocket these treasures, take them home and add them to his ever-growing collection of artifacts.

One day, when he was out exploring, John found more than just a trinket. Behind some rocks in a naturally occurring cave he found a rolled blanket. After staring at his unusual find for some time, the child's curiosity got the best of him and John unrolled the blanket. When he had the sheet open, he could hardly believe his eyes. There, before him, lay a perfectly formed skeleton— adorned only by a necklace. "The nicest blue bead necklace you ever saw," according to what John remembered years later.

Without so much as a thought, the boy slipped the piece of jewelry off the area between the body's chin and collarbone. He tucked his stolen treasure in his pocket and ran home. Although he was just a little boy, something in his being must have known that he'd done the wrong thing, for he hid the necklace that he'd found so attractive in a drawer and never said a word to anyone about his new possession.

That night he had a terrible nightmare. In his dream he saw the angry face of a Native woman coming at him. He could not see her body because it was wrapped in a blanket—a blanket that John Young recognized. It was the blanket that he had unwrapped from the skeleton that morning.

Not surprisingly, John shrieked in horror. As soon as he did the image disappeared.

Night after night the horror recurred in the youth's dreams. Then things began to go wrong for him during the day as well. Finally when an old, nearly lame horse that had been in his family for years charged at him and he nearly cut a finger off while chopping wood, the boy decided that the only way to bring peace back to his life was to return the necklace. He hiked out to the cave in the mountainside with the jewelry in his pocket. As quickly as he possibly could, John put the necklace back from where he'd stolen it in the first place.

John Young's nightmares and "accidents" stopped immediately, and the boy grew into an adult. He was always extremely careful to show respect for the rights of others, dead or alive.

5
Ghosts in Public

Do you think ghosts walk among us?
If not, perhaps the following stories might
change your opinion.

Bogeys in the Bakery

The bakery where Shawna worked during the mid-1990s in Bigfork, Montana, was a popular place. The shop not only sold baked goods but also served beverages and light meals. Customers and staff alike seemed friendly and upbeat. Shawna was sure she was going to enjoy working in such a lighthearted atmosphere. When one of her coworkers informed her that the building was haunted, the young woman took his "warning" to be nothing more serious than a tease.

She was a bit concerned, however, when she began to notice sparks of light flying about the shop. Thinking that her vision might simply have been affected by lack of sleep, Shawna didn't tell anyone about the strange things she'd seen. It wasn't until the first time she worked alone at night in the bakery that Shawna became convinced her coworker had not been teasing her. There certainly was a ghost in the bakery. She knew that because she'd seen the image for herself.

It was dark outside, but the bakery was well lit. As Shawna tidied up for the night, a movement in one of the glass cabinets caught her eye. At first all she could do was to stare in disbelief at the reflection looking back at her. She described the apparition as "resembling an old-time banker," complete with bowler hat, vest and watch fob. The vision was so lifelike that Shawna spun around, thinking that an oddly dressed customer must have come into the store, but no one was there. Glancing back at the glass on the front of the bakery display case, Shawna was shaken to see that the image was still there and that clearly it wasn't a reflection. There was no doubt in her mind—she was face to face with the spirit of a man—a man who had no doubt lived and died years before.

When she told her coworkers about the encounter, they were surprised—not that she'd seen a ghost but that the apparition appeared to be that of a man. Most of those who felt the spirit while they were working had been convinced that the ghost was that of a woman.

Some months after that experience, her first paranormal encounter, Shawna had to leave her job at the friendly but haunted bakery. As far as we know the ghost didn't follow her but has stayed behind at the retail outlet. It's reasonable to assume that, in life, the man had some association with the business or the building or at least the area. Unfortunately, we don't know for certain what his connection with the place might have been—perhaps he just loved baked goods!

Town Hall Haunted

By 1919, Littleton, Colorado, was already a thriving center. The community had long outgrown many of its public buildings, so the politicians, civil servants and citizens agreed to build new civic office facilities. Today that building might have been called a "multiplex," but in those days, Littletonians simply knew their town hall also, sensibly, housed the fire hall, the local jail and an area for community gathering.

Over the years the large brick building was the scene of many events—both positive and negative in nature. The town's politicians argued, its employees administered, its firemen stood on guard ready to protect the community full of wooden structures from fiery blazes and everyone, young and old alike, attended the dances held in the Littleton Town Hall. This sort of energy in and around a building often leaves the place haunted by the spirits of those who had been so dedicated to either the structure or its purpose. And according to some current-day reports, the post-World War I town hall in Littleton is no exception, for the building has been preserved and refurbished as an art gallery and a legitimate theater. As with many theaters (see my *Haunted Theaters*, Ghost House Books, 2002), ghosts apparently abound in the place.

The spirits populating the ethereal space in the Town Hall Arts Center are presumed to be those from the building's early days. Muffled noises, such as dance music, can be heard when there is no physical reason that there should be such sounds. It is likely that these phantom tunes are ghostly remains from the days when folks so enjoyed the dances held in the place. Apparently those partyers, now long dead, are still enjoying themselves, because their laughter and lively conversations still echo.

For the most part, today's employees at the center take the haunting in stride. Fundraiser Nancy Noyes, for instance, acknowledged to a journalist that the spirits were there but were not harmful. She described them as "whimsical," even though items on her desk would disappear or be rearranged when there was no one (no living person, that is) anywhere nearby.

In classic ghostly form, the spirits at the Arts Center like to ride up and down the elevator. While the building was completely secured, two people alone in the theater watched and listened in awe as the elevator began working. They were so surprised because no one was in the lift, and no one else was in any other part of the hall. The witnesses were sure of this because the sophisticated alarm system had been turned on and had not responded to any intruder. Because the alarm system was known to be trustworthy, the pair took immediate action and, like Elvis, they left the building!

If you visit Littleton, do stop by to admire the wonderfully preserved—and spirited—old building.

Haunted Ghost Town

Most of us enjoy exploring ghost towns—and it's really no wonder. Those long-deserted establishments are probably the closest any of us will ever get to taking a trip that includes time travel. With a bit of imagination, visiting a ghost town can transport you back to a way of life that existed a century or more before you were born. You can experience firsthand the feel of the dirt streets, the drafts coming in the cracks of the poorly constructed buildings and a sense of what life must have been like for the people who lived in the town when it was a viable community. In a few of these preserved old settlements, more than just the buildings remain. In some cases, such as the story that follows, even the spirits of those who lived in the town during its heyday have remained.

Most of these now-abandoned communities sprang to life as the search for gold moved westward. Prospectors struck a vein of ore, word of the cache quickly spread and, before long, the area would be flooded with thousands of prospective miners. Garnet, Montana (just west of Missoula) was one of those towns. It was settled in the 1860s and, like most gold rush towns, it was a tough place to live. Garnet was a place where disputes were customarily settled in very permanent ways, usually without benefit of the official legal system.

By the 1880s Garnet was every bit a typical boomtown. The gold strike had been exceptionally rich—there was gold for everyone, it seemed. The miners mined the gold in the hills, and the businesses mined the miners in town! Everyone was happy and making lots of money—for a while.

The specters of rugged miners still wander through Garnet, Montana, a historic ghost town.

Of course, the ore stores were not infinite, and before the turn of the last century, Garnet was all but empty. By the 1970s, some of the abandoned buildings still remained, but even they were collapsing from age and lack of maintenance. Fortunately, officials saw fit to restore the place so that people could experience, nearly firsthand, what the gold rush days were like. The project was a resounding success and has attracted many souls

202 Ghost Stories of the Rocky Mountains, Volume II

to Garnet's previously empty streets. Apparently the now-busy place hosts the spirits of the living and the souls of the dead. The revenants of yesterday's rough-and-tumble miners mingle with today's curious tourists.

During the days of the restoration, a worker named Kerry Moon attested that Garnet was a town that never really slept. Moon acknowledged that often in the day-time, as he looked down one of the main streets in the empty settlement, he could hear phantom sounds. He listened to horses' hooves clomping and wagon wheels crunching as they moved along the hard-packed dirt roads, although he couldn't see anything moving, certainly nothing that would have made such sounds.

The nights, though, were especially eerie. And of all the nights of the week, Wednesdays for some reason were the most active. Moon recalled watching in awe as lights came on in various "empty" buildings around Garnet. He could see silhouettes of those enjoying themselves and hear their music and their laughter. The noises were so real and so loud that some nights Moon and the other workers who were staying on the property could not get much sleep.

One winter night there was a persistent knocking on the door of the workers' dorm. When they answered the knocks there was no one there—and there were no footsteps in the freshly fallen snow.

The ghost of the town's former blacksmith almost never rested—he could be heard pounding on horseshoes long into the night, roughly a century after he died. And the place was also home to a honky-tonk pianist with similar tenacity. When the ghostly musician began playing in the middle of a severe snowstorm, Moon made his way through the drifts to see if somehow a real-life intruder had broken into the saloon. As Moon approached the building, he heard the pianist switch from song to song, but as he came close to the building the music abruptly stopped. Relieved and also considerably unnerved, Moon decided to return to his quarters. As he turned around and started to retreat from the downtown area, the music started up again. The man was alone in the ghost town, so he wisely decided to go to bed for the night and simply let the ghosts party in peace. But then his sense of responsibility eventually won out over his fear, and Moon trekked back to the saloon. He made his way inside the deserted building.

It was cold, dark and completely quiet in the building except for some intruders—in the form of pigeons. What startled Moon most, though, was the discovery that there was no piano in the saloon. He found out later that there hadn't been any musical instruments at all in that building for nearly 100 years. He had been hearing music that originated many, many years before and was being replayed on something of an infinite paranormal loop.

Fearing being labeled as untrustworthy and too imaginative, those stationed at Garnet, Moon included, kept the ghost stories from the ghost town to themselves for many years. By now so many people have encountered the ghostly activity in the ghost town that the presence of the spirits is well accepted—by even the most skeptical.

A Final Farewell

Children often share a very special relationship with their grandparents. As we will see in the next story, sometimes that bond extends across the great beyond.

Twelve-year-old Vicki lived in west-central Montana in the Deer Lodge area, when her maternal grandfather, Dyer, passed away. The man's death was a considerable loss to the entire family. From their descriptions it would seem that Dyer had been a pivotal member of the clan.

The night after Dyer's death, Vicki, her siblings and their parents were in their beds sleeping when they were awakened by the sounds of heavy footsteps in the house. The parents knew these sounds were too heavy to have been made by one of the children, so they got up to check on what was happening. When they got to the doorway leading from the living room to the kitchen, they were relieved to note that there was no intruder, but they were rather shocked to see a mysterious white vapor before them.

As they stared into the kitchen they heard some noise, a man's voice, coming from the strange mist. It seemed that the voice was in a conversation with someone neither Vicki's mother nor father could see. Seconds later the young mother whispered nervously into her husband's ear, "I think that's my father talking."

The children continued to sleep until the presence entered their room. That was when Vicki felt a comforting hand on her shoulder and then someone sit down on the bed beside her. The sensations were so real that she was sure it was her younger brother wanting to get into bed with her. Vicki opened her eyes and pulled back the covers to let the little boy under the sheets. But there was no little boy there; there was only a white misty fog and the clear impression that her grandfather was nearby.

The following morning at breakfast the family compared stories about their experiences the night before. It seemed that the previous night Dyer's image had visited everyone in the house, at least for a while. Later on in the day they also learned that he had visited other family members that night—people who lived many miles away. And, impossibly, he visited them at exactly the same moment he visited Vicki's household.

The following night, the spirit visited his widow before saying good-bye and never again returning to this side of the curtain of time.

Bookstore Bogey

Used bookstores are very special places. Where else could a bookworm find such treats as an original edition of a favorite childhood novel or an obscure out-of-print text that would be the perfect gift for a friend?

These treasure-trove shops often seem to be halfway between an old-fashioned library and a well-stocked independent bookstore selling new releases. Customers can sit surrounded by the wisdom of the ages enjoying the comfort of an overstuffed chair, the slightly musty aroma of the old books and possibly even a cup of freshly brewed coffee.

In addition to being able to count on those inviting qualities in a used bookstore, it's usually a pretty fair bet that the shop's owner is a middle-aged person with at least slightly left-leaning political views.

Oh yes, and wouldn't it just complete this picture if the overflowing shelves and narrow aisles were haunted?

Jeff Toten, who owns Old Possum Books, a well-stocked emporium of reading delights in Broomfield, Colorado, is not a middle-aged man but a young one, and he describes his political views as decidedly "hardcore."

Jeff explains, "I'm different than most of your used bookstore owners because I'm very conservative. I served in the military. I served in combat. I'm definitely more hardcore than anything else. Things just don't bother me that much. Things don't usually scare me but this one did. Every once in a while it gave me chills."

As far as belief in the paranormal goes, Jeff had always considered himself a skeptic. Fortunately for ghost story lovers and unfortunately for Jeff's nervous system, the manifestation that haunted his store did a very effective job changing the young man's beliefs.

In the fall of 2002, Jeff generously chatted at length about the store, the strange activities there and what it was that altered his attitude toward the supernatural. He explained it this way: "I don't really believe in ghosts necessarily but if I look at everything I've been through I'd have to say 'okay.' "

And so, over the period of the haunting, Jeff slowly, and a bit grudgingly, lost his skepticism.

"My wife, Bonnie, and I started this bookstore in 1997. We chose a location in the old section of Broomfield, Colorado. This building, though, was actually fairly new—built in 1972. Now as far as I know, there's no real history about the building itself. Back in the 1900s, though, there was a bar on this lot and I understand there were lots of 'dens of iniquity' in the neighborhood."

The history of the land could have contributed to the supernatural interference Jeff and his wife met with when they began their business endeavor. There are certainly other possibilities as well—for example, used books have had ample opportunities to pick up ghostly energies of their own. It's foolish, therefore, to jump to any definitive conclusions.

From the tone of his voice, it was evident that talking about the supernatural events that occurred in his workplace brought back Jeff's feelings of discomfort. He acknowledged, "You're actually the first person who's ever talked to me about the haunting—for publication anyway. I've told very few people about this."

With that initial hesitancy out of the way, Jeff proceeded to explain how the ghost had made its presence known.

"When we opened the store, we had all of our books up on the shelves. We also put an antique oak library ladder in. Near that ladder there's now a door. It had been plastered over but there had been a doorway there originally and we reopened it."

Jeff reminded me that "all of the books were up on the shelves," and then he went on to describe his first encounter with the actions of the resident specter.

"When I'd come here in the morning I always felt just a little odd—you know that feeling when the hairs stand up on the back of your neck? I'd get that but I wouldn't think anything of it. I'd come in and find three or four paperback books lying on the floor in different aisles. It was like someone had pulled them off the shelf and then just dropped them. That happened not just once or twice. It happened several times."

Trying to convince himself that something completely explainable was at work, Jeff wondered if trucks rumbling along on the road outside had caused vibrations that knocked the books off the shelves and onto the floor. He really didn't have much luck selling that theory to himself, however, and when the haunting increased in strength, he just couldn't rationalize away the bizarre occurrences that were happening.

"When I was here sitting at my desk working on the laptop computer, I heard books fall. They'd fallen from the history section. Four books fell off three different shelves. They didn't hit each other going down, that's for sure. That incident really sent chills up my spine because the store was completely empty at the time except for me."

Jeff's firmly resolved skepticism was understandably beginning to weaken. "A few times I was up on top of the oak ladder with books stacked beside me. The books would actually fall off the ladder. I've never been able to come up with an explanation for that."

These sorts of mysterious and unnerving events continued to occur in Old Possum Books for the next two years. Jeff was just getting somewhat used to the activity when the resident spirit tried another trick.

One day a customer was sitting relaxing and reading. "She was in plain view," the proprietor assured me before continuing with his explanation. "I heard something that sounded like somebody knocking on a piece of wood. It was loud but it was coming from the back room, completely opposite of where this woman was sitting. I looked up and I looked back and I saw the woman sitting there. She was still reading a book, so I went back to work on my computer. Then I heard three more knocks, and again I turned around and looked, but she was still there reading a book so it clearly wasn't her making the knocking sounds."

Jeff turned away to face the front of the store but that didn't help him feel comfortable at all. "I had the strangest sensation that somebody was right behind me, right there looking at me."

By this point in the conversation I could feel Jeff's emotional reaction to that uncomfortable feeling he'd had. I was just about to express that to him when his voice went up noticeably and he exclaimed, "I just got a cold chill telling you about it."

I might have guessed that Jeff was simply reacting to the strange memory, that explaining the situation to me had brought the incident back to the forefront of his mind. Unfortunately for my own comfort level, however, at exactly that point in the call there was an unusual clicking noise on the phone line. This struck me as an odd coincidence but I didn't say anything to Jeff. I certainly didn't want to risk not hearing the rest of this intriguing tale.

He continued to describe the scene: "I turned around really quickly but there was no one there and the woman was still sitting there reading her book."

Jeff remembers that he had become completely exasperated with the phantom knocking that was disturbing the tranquility in the store. "I just said out loud, 'Oh, give me a break!' The feeling left me immediately."

That certainly didn't mean that the store became a ghost-free zone. Even though Jeff never spoke of the haunting, others were soon picking up on the presence of an otherworldly entity in the store.

Jeff explained, "I would have friends over and I'd have all the lights turned on in the store but still people would get the 'willies.' They'd say, 'There's something in that back aisle.' "

Jeff always agreed with his friends that there was something unusual about the atmosphere in the store because he felt it too. "I would go to the room farthest back and for the longest time whenever I was back there I would get a really strange sensation. For a while I just didn't like being there because it felt really bad. I didn't want to stay there too long."

Jeff's wife was even more bothered by the creepy sensations. As a result, in order to run the business and work around the haunting, they chose to try to ignore the inexplicable activities. "We just kind of let it be" is how he described the attitudes they adopted.

Shortly after Jeff asked the spirits to give him a break, they did. He reported that since then, "I haven't had any books winding up in the middle of the floor ever again. Books haven't been jumping off the shelf. I haven't had that problem since. Everything that I'm doing is the same as what I'd been doing in the past. Nothing has changed, so it leads me to say that something was here."

The welcome peace and quiet may not have been a reaction to the man's plea, though, but a result of a sadder incident.

"My wife suddenly passed away two years ago. Since then even that strange sensation in the back of the room is gone. I don't know if Bonnie came back and kicked the spirit's butt. I could feel Bonnie here for a long time but I don't feel her around here anymore either. It took about nine months after her death but now I'm not bothered any longer by any presences—not that I know of, anyway."

Now that Jeff works without invisible entities surrounding him, he feels more free to speculate on what or who could have caused the haunting.

"I do connect this with the history of the land. Broomfield is located between Boulder and Denver and there are Louisville and Lafayette too. These three areas were huge into coal mining so there's a lot of history here. Jeff paused for a moment before continuing to postulate. "Or, it could be that some [supernatural] energy came in on some books. That could be it. But, I haven't really felt any presences here lately. Just every once in a while I'll feel something but nothing compared to what the haunting was like. In fact I live here in the store now. If there's anybody here we get along just fine now. I haven't had any bad things happen around here."

And so, Jeff's life continues and his business prospers as a result of hard work and support from friends and family who are very much alive. Only time will tell for certain whether the ghosts are gone forever or are, for the time being, just keeping a low profile. Either way, a visit to Old Possum Books in Broomfield, Colorado, is a great place to stock up on some spirited reading material.

Evil Predictor

Ships, the sea and ghost lore have a long association with one another. Sailors are extremely superstitious, and many of their beliefs include tales about ghosts.

The sheer numbers of these sorts of legends have led us to expect that paranormal nautical tales will be included in any book containing ghost stories from a Maritime location. However, we don't normally expect to find such articles in a book about ghosts of the Rocky Mountains. Even so, the following true story is just exactly that—an account of a ghost ship seen on the Platte River, roughly 6 miles (10 kilometers) southeast of Guernsey, Wyoming.

A ghost ship (sometimes called a Flying Dutchman or a phantom ship) is an apparition of a vessel that no longer exists. Most commonly, these sightings are reported at the place where that particular vessel sank. Such visions almost always foretell tragedy. The phantom ship of Platte River is such a predictive and foreboding sight that the ghost has come to be known as "The Ship of Death."

No one knows when the ship, in its physical form, actually sailed Wyoming's grand Platte River. The first recorded sighting of its spectral image occurred in the early autumn of 1862, when a trapper named Leon Weber stood on the riverbank awaiting the arrival of his bride-to-be.

The vessel that came toward him was certainly not where he was expecting to see his beloved. Far from it. The ship before his eyes was old, rotting and dilapidated—a disgusting sight. Anyone who ever saw this phantom ship was terrified of it.

The dreadful image always emerges from a localized mist—a fog some have described as "unnatural." The few sails that remain on the riggings are torn and filthy. The apparitions of the crew members, a motley-looking lot, are apparently even more unnerving. Weber, for instance, knew immediately that neither the vessel nor the people were of this world, for he could see right through them. These ghastly specters always gather at a particular area of the ship's deck. And they always gather around a corpse.

When Leon Weber saw the tragic omen with his own eyes, a cold shiver ran through his entire body. He knew this was a prophecy. The corpse on the deck of the phantom ship was the image of Margaret Stanley, his beloved fiancée.

He learned later that Margaret, who had been in perfect health, had died unexpectedly that afternoon. The eerie omen of the phantom ship had been accurate.

Twenty-five years later, Gene Wilson, a local rancher, also saw the grisly craft—this time the woman aboard was not Leon Weber's girlfriend but Wilson's own wife, who was healthy and vibrant when Wilson had seen her just hours before. Wilson rushed home immediately. He found his wife's body by the riverbank. Mrs. Wilson had burned to death. Sometime later, Gene Wilson speculated that his wife's clothes might have caught on fire from a spark from the wood stove and that the terrified woman had probably headed to the river in hopes of drowning the flames. Unfortunately, she didn't make it to the water in time and she died—at exactly the moment that the phantom ship had appeared to her husband.

Another documented sighting of the horrid, rotting boat occurred in 1903 when a man named Victor Heibe spotted the phantom ship and his friend, who seemed to be aboard it. Hiebe's friend died shortly after the precognitive signal was seen.

A further twist in this phantom ship story—aside from its extremely unusual location in Wyoming—is that these sightings are only ever witnessed in autumn, never in spring, summer or winter.

Although it's difficult to understand why anyone would want to see this particular ghost, as it is a harbinger of death, some people are apparently interested. With the upsurge in curiosity about ghosts, industrious folks in many haunted areas of the world have created location-specific ghost tours. One of those tours includes the very spot along the Platte River where the manifestation is known to appear. Several groups of ghost hunters have apparently seen the frightening image. Fortunately there have been no reports of any tragedies immediately befalling any of the witnesses. Despite that, it is probably wise not to go looking for this particular ghostly image—especially not in autumn.

THE END

Enjoy more terrifying tales in these collections!

GHOST HOUSE BOOKS

The colorful history of North America includes many spine-tingling tales of the supernatural. These fun, fascinating collections from Ghost House Books reveal the rich diversity of haunted places on the continent. Our ghostly tales involve well-known theaters, buildings and other landmarks, many of which are still in use. Collect the whole series!

Ghost Stories of the Sea *by Barbara Smith*

Ghosts and the sea are each mysterious. Combined, they are nearly irresistible for those who love to explore the unknown. Barbara Smith explores the haunting tales from ships past and present, including USS *The Sullivans,* the *Queen Mary* and the *Mary Celeste.*

$10.95US/$14.95CDN • ISBN 1-894877-23-3 • 5.25" x 8.25" • 224 pages

Haunted Highways *by Dan Asfar*

Lights on the road. Ghost hitchhikers. Eerie covered bridges. Dan Asfar shows how some of America's most innocuous streets and thoroughfares can suddenly become terrifying haunts.

$10.95US/$14.95CDN • ISBN 1-894877-29-2 • 5.25" x 8.25" • 224 pages

Haunted Schools *by A.S. Mott*

Schools are centers of learning, respected for their rational approach to the world we live in. But many of North America's schools are also hotbeds of the unexplained, where ghosts terrify the living with lessons they won't forget.

$10.95US/$14.95CDN • ISBN 1-894877-32-2 • 5.25" x 8.25" • 216 pages

Also look for

Ghost Stories of the Rocky Mountains *by Barbara Smith*	ISBN 1-55105-165-6
Haunted Hotels *by Jo-Anne Christensen*	ISBN 1-894877-03-9
Haunted Theaters *by Barbara Smith*	ISBN 1-894877-04-7
Campfire Ghost Stories *by Jo-Anne Christensen*	ISBN 1-894877-02-0

These and many more Ghost House books are available from your local bookseller or by ordering direct. U.S. readers call 1-800-518-3541. In Canada, call 1-800-661-9017.